Apologia for Tradition

APOLOGIA FOR TRADITION

A defense of Tradition grounded in
the historical context of the Faith

ROBERTO DE MATTEI

Foreword by Peter A. Kwasniewski

Translated by Michael J. Miller

2915 Forest Avenue | Kansas City, MO 64109

Original edition: *Apologia della Tradizione: Poscritto a "Il Concilio Vaticano II. Una storia mai scritta"* © 2011 Lindau s.r.l. Corso Re Umberto 37 – 10128 Torino (Turin), ITALY

Cover: Giovanni Ambrogio Figino (c. 1590). *Sant'Ambrogio a cavallo scaccia gli ariani* [*St. Ambrose on horseback driving out the Arians*]. Pinacoteca del Castello Sforzesco, Milano. Copyright Comune di Milano, tutti i diritti riservati.

Library of Congress Cataloging-in-Publication Data

Names: De Mattei, Roberto, author. | Miller, Michael J., translator.
Title: Apologia for tradition : a defense of tradition grounded in the historical context of the faith / Roberto de Mattei ; translated by Michael J. Miller.
Other titles: Apologia della tradizione. English
Description: Kansas City, MO : Angelus Press, 2019. | Translation of: Apologia della Tradizione. | Includes bibliographical references and index.
Identifiers: LCCN 2018061278 | ISBN 9781949124033 (pbk. : alk. paper)
Subjects: LCSH: Tradition (Theology) | Church history. | Catholic Church--History. | Vatican Council (2nd : 1962-1965 : Basilica di San Pietro in Vaticano)--History.
Classification: LCC BT90 .D4213 2019 | DDC 231/.042--dc23
LC record available at https://lccn.loc.gov/2018061278

©2019 by Angelus Press

All rights reserved. No part of this book may be reproduced or transmitted in any form or by any means, electronic or mechanical, including photocopying, recording, or by any information storage and retrieval systems without permission in writing from the publisher, except by a reviewer, who may quote brief passages in a review.

ANGELUS PRESS
2915 FOREST AVENUE
KANSAS CITY, MISSOURI 64109
PHONE (816) 753-3150
ORDER LINE 1-800-966-7337
www.angeluspress.org

ISBN: 978-1-949124-03-3
First Printing—March 2019

Printed in the United States of America

Table of Contents

Abbreviations of Works Cited vii
Foreword. ix
Introduction 1

I The Church Militant in the Most Difficult Hours of Its History

1. The era of persecutions 11
2. The Arian crisis in the fourth century. 13
3. Shadows and highlights of the first Councils. 18
4. *"Error cui non resistitur approbatur"* .23
5. When the philosophy of the Gospel governed the States 27
6. The Avignon crisis and the "Great Western Schism" 34
7. The Councils of the 15th Century .38
8. From humanism to Protestantism 42
9. The failed reform of Hadrian VI. 46
10. From the Council of Trent to the French Revolution 49
11. From Blessed Pius IX to St. Pius X .55
12. The rock of Peter overcomes every storm. 58

II The Church's *Regula Fidei* in Times of Crises of Faith

1. Benedict XVI and the hermeneutic of continuity 61
2. The method of "the sources of theology". 64
3. The primacy of Sacred Tradition. 67
4. The Church and her spirit of truth 68
5. The absence of the Magisterium from the theological sources 69
6. What is Tradition? 71
7. Tradition and the Church 75
8. The Church, the Mystical Body of Christ 77
9. The authority of the Magisterium 79
10. Tradition and the Magisterium 80
11. The criterion of Tradition 81
12. Teaching Church and learning Church. 85
13. The active and passive infallibility of the Church 86
14. The Christian sense of faith 87

15. *Sensus fidei* and Tradition.................................. 90
16. *Sensus fidei* and resistance to the ecclesiastical authorities... 94
17. Infallibility of Councils? 97
18. The Meaning of "Universal Magisterium"..............101
19. Novelties or development in doctrine?................105
20. Vatican Council II and its problems..................106
21. The Council in the light of Tradition.................109
22. Apologia for Tradition 112

Index of Names................................... 115

Abbreviations of Works Cited

AAS (ASS before 1909): *Acta Apostolicae Sedis* (Vatican City: Typis Vaticana, 1909 ff.).

ANF: *Ante-Nicene Fathers*, American edition, 10 vols. (Christian Literature Publishing Company, 1885 ff.; Hendrickson Publishers, 1994).

Benedetto XVI, *Insegnamenti: Insegnamenti di Benedetto XVI* (Vatican City: Libreria Editrice Vaticana, 2006 ff.).

CIC: *The Code of Canon Law in English Translation* (London: Collins Liturgical Publications/William B. Eerdmans Publishing Company, 1983).

COD: *Conciliorum Oecumenicorum Decreta*, bilingual Italian edition by the Istituto per le Scienze Religiose (Bologna: EDB, 2002).

DBI: *Dizionario Biografico degli Italiani* (Rome: Istituto dell'Enciclopedia Italiana, 1960 ff.).

DH: Heinrich Denzinger, *Enchiridion Symbolorum definitionum et declarationum de rebus fidei et morum*, ed. Peter Hünermann, 43rd edition, Latin-English edition edited by Robert Fastiggi and Anne Englund Nash (San Francisco: Ignatius Press, 2012).

DHGE: *Dictionnaire d'Histoire et de Géographie Ecclésiastiques* (Paris: Letouzey et Ané, 1912 ff.).

DSP: *Dizionario Storico del Papato*, 2 vols. (Milan: Bompiani, 1996).

DTC: *Dictionnaire de Théologie Catholique*, ed. A. Vacant and E. Mangenot, 33 vols. (Paris: Letouzey et Ané, 1909-1972).

EC: *Enciclopedia Cattolica*, 12 vols. (Florence: Sansoni, 1949-1954).

EE: *Enchiridion delle Encicliche*, bilingual (Italian) edition (Bologna: EDB, 1995-1999).

Ench. Conc.: *Enchiridion dei Concordati: Due secoli dei rapport Chiesa-Stato* (Bologna: EDB, 2003).

EP: *Enciclopedia dei Papi*, vol. III (Rome: Istituto della Enciclopedia Italiana, 2000).

Hergenröther: Joseph Hergenröther, *Storia universale della Chiesa* fourth edition revised by Monsignor G. P. Kirsch, Italian translation by Fr. Enrico Rosa, S.J., 7 vols. (Florence: Libreria Editrice Fiorentina, 1907-1911).

John Paul II, *Insegnamenti: Insegnamenti di Giovanni Paolo II* (Vatican City: Libreria Editrice Vaticana, 1980 ff.).

La Chiesa: in *Insegnamenti Pontifici*, edited by the Benedictine Monks of Solesmes, 2 vols. (Rome: Paoline, 1971).

LTK: *Lexikon für Theologie und Kirche*, 10 vols. (Freiburg im Breisgau: Herder, 1957-1965).

Mansi: Giovanni Domenico Mansi, *Sacrorum conciliorum nova et amplissima Collectio*, ed. Louis Petit and Jean-Baptiste Martin, 53 vols. (Paris-Arnhem-Leipzig, 1901-1927).

NPNF-1: *Nicene and Post-Nicene Fathers – First Series*, American edition, 14 vols. (Christian Literature Publishing Company, 1886 ff.; Hendrickson Publishers, 1994).

NPNF-2: *Nicene and Post-Nicene Fathers – Second Series*, American edition, 14 vols. (Christian Literature Publishing Company, 1890 ff.; Hendrickson Publishers, 1994).

Paul VI, *Insegnamenti:* Paolo VI, *Insegnamenti*, 16 vols. (Vatican City: Tipografia Poliglotta Vaticana, 1963-1978).

Pastor: Ludwig von Pastor, *Storia dei Papa dalla fine del Medioevo*, 16 vols. (Rome: Desclée & C., 1926-1963).

PG: *Patrologiae Cursus Completus, Series Graeca*, ed. Jean-Paul Migne, 221 vols. (Paris: 1844-1864).

Pius XII, DRM: Pio XII, *Discorsi e Radiomessaggi*, 21 vols. (Vatican City: Tipografia Poliglotta Vaticana, 1959).

PL: *Patrologiae Cursus Completus, Series Latina*, ed. Jean-Paul Migne, 226 vols. (Paris: 1844-1864).

Foreword

It would once have caused no raising of eyebrows to state that Catholicism is inherently a religion of tradition. This was one of the main objections raised against it by Protestants, who, having settled on the doctrine of *sola scriptura,* discovered unsurprisingly that much of what the Catholic Church taught and practiced could not be found *verbatim* in the Bible. Yet, this discovery should not have startled followers of the Apostle St. Paul, who wrote to the Corinthians: "I commend you because you remember me in everything and maintain the traditions even as I have delivered them to you" (I Cor. 11:2), and to the Thessalonians: "So then, brethren, stand firm and hold to the traditions which you were taught by us, either by word of mouth or by letter" (II Thess. 2:15).

The Church Fathers drove this point home with their customary vehemence. In his treatise *On the Holy Spirit,* published in 375, St. Basil the Great tells us:

> Of the dogmas and messages preserved in the Church, some we possess from written teaching and others we receive from the tradition of the apostles, handed on to us in mystery. In respect to piety, both are of the same force. No one will contradict any of these—no one, at any rate, who is even moderately versed in ecclesiastical matters. Indeed, were we to try to reject unwritten customs as having no great authority, we would unwittingly injure the Gospel in its vitals.

St. Basil helpfully tells us the sort of thing he has in mind, and if we listen carefully, we will hear some examples that may surprise us:

> To take the first and most general example, who is there who has taught us in writing to sign with the sign of the Cross those who have trusted in the name of Our Lord Jesus Christ? What writing has taught us to turn to the East at the [Eucharistic] prayer? Which of the saints has left us in writing the words of the invocation at the displaying of the bread of the Eucharist and the cup of blessing? For we are not, as is well known, content with what the Apostle or the Gospel has recorded, but both in preface and conclusion we add other words as being of great importance to the validity of the ministry, and these we derive from unwritten teaching. Moreover, we bless the water of baptism and the oil of chrism, and besides this the catechumen who is being baptized. On what written authority do we do this? Is not our authority silent and mystical tradition? Nay, by

what written word is the anointing of oil itself taught? And whence comes the custom of baptizing thrice? And as to the other customs of baptism, from what Scripture do we derive the renunciation of Satan and his angels? Does not this come from that unpublished and secret teaching which our fathers guarded in a silence out of the reach of curious meddling and inquisitive investigation? Well had they learnt the lesson that the awful dignity of the mysteries is best preserved by silence. What the uninitiated are not even allowed to look at was hardly likely to be publicly paraded about in written documents.

Another Church Father, St. Vincent of Lérins, around the year 434, had this to say in his great treatise *Commonitory for the Antiquity and Universality of the Catholic Faith Against the Profane Novelties of All Heresies*:

> *Keep the deposit.* What is the deposit? That which has been entrusted to you, not that which you have yourself devised: a matter not of cleverness, but of learning; not of private adoption, but of public tradition; a matter brought to you, not put forth by you, wherein you are bound to be not an author but a keeper, not a teacher but a disciple, not a leader but a follower. *Keep the deposit.* Preserve the talent of Catholic Faith inviolate, unadulterate. That which has been entrusted to you, let it continue in your possession, let it be handed on by you. You have received gold; give gold in turn. Do not substitute one thing for another. Do not for gold impudently substitute lead or brass. Give real gold, not counterfeit.

Such quotations could be multiplied indefinitely. The Church Fathers saw Christianity as a social and hierarchical religion in which certain men—the apostles and their successors—had been entrusted with dogmas, liturgical practices, and moral judgments that were intended to be passed on faithfully from one generation to the next. And this is a key point: the doctrine revealed by God, *in its totality,* was first deposited in *tradition,* that is, in the minds of the men whom God had chosen as His confidantes, and only subsequently was *some* of it placed in writing, at the discretion of the ones to whom the deposit had been given. We have to get away from any notion of a Bible, a catechism, or a *Summa* falling from the sky into the hands of prophets or apostles. Revelation is a definite spiritual light that God plants in the minds of His instruments, entrusting them with the task of explaining it in their spoken words and putting some portion of it into writing for the benefit of distant or future audiences. But it is clear that it would have been impossible to put *all* of it into writing: St. John tells us in Chapter 21 of his Gospel: "There are also many other things which Jesus did; which, if they were written every one, the world itself, I think, would not be able to contain the books that should be written." Neither the apostles nor the Church Fathers felt that they *should* or *could* put into writing all that belonged to the mystery of life in Christ. The Church preserves in her maternal heart some memories that are too deep for words, and some realities that find their expression in signs and symbols rather than in written language.

The Catholic Faith is not just bound up with tradition, it actually exists *in the mode of tradition*—that is, in the mode of something handed down; and this is the only way in which it lives and moves and has its being. Just as Almighty God saved us not by means of an abstract metaphysical system but through a messy and lengthy history, so too, he established the Catholic Church and its doctrine and life as a reality entrusted to the apostles and transmitted, by them, to succeeding generations. While one can have a catechism that reads as if it fell from the heavens with an objective and timeless content (a style highly appropriate for a catechism, no doubt), the Faith is a living reality put into certain peoples' hands and handed over by them to us who now believe. In a broad sense, the entirety of revelation—including Scripture—is part of tradition. Scripture, too, has been delivered to the Church and handed down by her to us.

This transmission is integral, complete, undistorted, and essentially unchanging, as St. Vincent of Lérins sees it. Blessed John Henry Newman shows with rigorous reasoning how the legitimate developments that have occurred historically affected not the body of the truth but, as it were, its clothing, or put differently, not the truth of the word but the fullness of its verbal expression. While the crisis of modernism can be understood in many ways, it seems to me that the crux of the matter is an adoption of a Hegelian (although one might just as easily say Darwinian or Marxist) understanding of development of doctrine: what we believe *now* and how we practice and pray are *different* from what they used to be, simply because our *age* is different—our experiences, feelings, mentality, and science are different. The traditional Catholic decisively rejects this Hegelian deception and affirms the Vincentian/Newmanian unity of revelation *as handed down over time,* with the guidance of the Holy Spirit leading the Church into the full expression of revealed truth.

Once one grants that there is an integral truth handed down over the centuries and developed organically, then it must be possible for deviation and corruption to set in because of the sins of Christians, and particularly wayward shepherds. Heresy is always possible; misunderstanding, distortion, overemphasis, underemphasis, secularization, all of these things can happen, and when they happen, they begin to undermine "the Faith once delivered to the saints" in the souls of individuals who are not strong in the knowledge and practice of the Faith—including members of the Church hierarchy. This was seen most famously in England at the time of the Reformation, when all the bishops except St. John Fisher went along with King Henry VIII's machinations. We see it today in the clear split between the bishops who accept and teach authentic Catholic doctrine on marriage and family and those who do not, or (to take a random example) between bishops who know and clearly state that the Catholic Church is the one true Church of Christ to which all Protestants are called by God to return, and those who counsel people to remain in their objectively heretical or schismatic positions either temporarily or permanently.

Here there arises a point that distinguishes traditionalists from other Catholics. The traditionalist would say that it is possible—and indeed it has really happened—that a pope or a Council could introduce language or liturgy that departs from the constancy, integrity, and purity of the apostolic tradition in its organic development, not in such a way that dogma is contradicted or sin prescribed, but in such a way that dogmas are confused, errors invited, and deviations disseminated. If such a thing has taken place, the solution is not to throw overboard that which is ancient, venerable, and constant, but to judge as inadequate and dangerous that which departs from it, and to hold fast to the tried and true.

Considering the immense importance of tradition as Catholics understand it, one must be surprised, if not bewildered, by the lack of suitable treatments of the subject, particularly in the period following the Second Vatican Council. It is almost as if that "supercouncil" had erased the very notion and need of tradition by creating a new "pastoral theology" *ex nihilo* that operates in its own abstract framework.

This outstanding book by esteemed Professor Roberto de Mattei therefore comes not a moment too soon. Overcoming the terrible neglect of a reality at the very heart of Christianity, *Apologia for Tradition* has the great and singular merit of immersing the reader deeply in this rich reality, which illuminates not only all that the Church has been and must be, but also how we are to respond to the crisis of increasing obfuscation as the clouds of a pseudo-magisterium close densely around the sun of truth. We have long been in Professor de Mattei's debt for his groundbreaking research on the last Council and for his host of articles and speeches on contemporary Catholic issues. With this book, de Mattei has given us a most valuable and timely resource for grasping what is at stake in the dynamics and direction of Catholicism today. May it be read as widely as its accuracy and wisdom merit.

Peter A. Kwasniewski, Ph.D.
October 24, 2018
Feast of St. Raphael Archangel

Introduction

In his address to the Roman Curia on December 20, 2010,[1] Benedict XVI compared the crisis of our time to the one in the 5th century after Christ which witnessed the decline and fall of the Roman Empire.

The analogies between the two eras are real: whereas the Roman Empire fell because of barbarian invasions, but above all as a result of its interior decomposition. Today too our civilization is subjected to growing pressure from outside while it suffers internally from a situation of cultural and moral disintegration.

And nevertheless, there is a fundamental difference between the conditions in the society of that time and those of the contemporary Western world. In the Dark Ages of the barbarian invasions, between the 5th and 6th centuries, when political and social institutions were collapsing, the Catholic Church asserted herself as the sole center of order and stability in the general chaos. The names of St. Leo and of St. Gregory, popes to whom the Church has attributed the title of "Great," remind us of the decisive role that the papal institution played in those centuries.

Today, the Church is under attack and appears to be suffering and weakened. She does not stand firm, as she did in the 5th century, above the breakers of history, but seems as if swept away by them; the whirlpool of self-destruction is tearing her apart,[2] and by the admission of her own highest authorities, she is going through one of the most severe internal crises of her existence.[3]

This crisis had a focal point in the Second Vatican Council held in Rome between October 1962 and December 1965. From then on the Church seems to have allowed herself to be seduced by the

---

[1] Benedict XVI, Address to the Roman Curia, December 20, 2010, in http://w2.vatican.va/content/benedict-xvi/en/speeches/2010/december/documents/hf_ben-xvi_spe_20101220_curia-auguri.html.

[2] Cardinal Joseph Ratzinger himself spoke about the Church that was "tearing herself apart" in *Milestones: Memoirs: 1927-1977* (San Francisco: Ignatius Press, 1998), 149.

[3] See, for example, Paul VI, Conversation with the graduates of the Pontifical Lombard Seminary (December 7, 1968), in *Insegnamenti* 6:1187-1189 at 1188, and John Paul II, Address to Religious and Priests (February 6, 1981), in *Insegnamenti*, 4:233-237 at 235.

modern world, which she ought to have opposed actively, and today she struggles in its lethal embrace.

Benedict XVI, who experienced the years of the Council as one of its young leading figures and then, as Prefect of the Congregation for the Doctrine of the Faith, was able to assess the depth and the extent of the post-conciliar crisis, is aware more than anyone else of the tragic implications of the problem. In a famous address, the one given to the Roman Curia on December 22, 2005,[4] he proposed using the method of the "hermeneutic of continuity" as opposed to the hermeneutic of discontinuity and rupture. In doing so, Benedict XVI in fact subjected Vatican Council II both to theological reflection and to historical discussion.

This means that in studying the Council, besides the hermeneutical work of theologians, it is necessary for historians to reconstruct the facts, their roots and their consequences. This is what I sought to do in my book *The Second Vatican Council (an unwritten story)*: a historical reconstruction that was as truthful and faithful as possible to the conciliar event, based on the sources and on the documents.[5]

Although the critiques of my book thus far have been few and not very substantial, I think that is it useful to offer a few points of reflection to those who want to study in greater depth the problems inevitably raised by it, and in particular this one: can we discuss Vatican Council II historically, bringing to light possible shadows, limits and negative consequences? And, more generally, is it legitimate for the historian to point out and possibly to criticize ecclesiastical persons and events?

Answers to these questions can be given on two levels, the historical and the theological. The important thing is not to superimpose the two areas, which are neither separate nor sealed off from each other, yet certainly remain distinct: history and theology. History,

---

[4] Benedict XVI, Address to the Roman Curia, December 22, 2005. https://w2.vatican.va/content/benedict-xvi/en/speeches/2005/december/documents/hf_ben_xvi_spe_20051222_roman-curia.html.

[5] *Il Concilio Vaticano II: Una storia mai scritta* (Turin: Lindau, 2010). English edition: *The Second Vatican Council (an unwritten story)*, translated by Michael J. Miller *et al.* (Fitzwilliam, NH, 2012). For a theological and philosophical reflection on Vatican Council II, see also the works by Romano Amerio, *Iota unum* (Kansas City, MO: Sarto House, 1996); Monsignor Brunero Gherardini, *The Ecumenical Vatican Council: A Much Needed Discussion* (Frigento: Casa Mariana Editrice, 2009), and *idem, Un concilio mancato* (Turin: Lindau, 2011).

nevertheless, is not a mere exposition of facts but an authentic "knowledge" directed toward reconstructing events in an orderly manner, by means of value judgments, after having weighed the reliability of the documents and testimonies. In the case of the history of the Church, Monsignor Hubert Jedin observes, it receives the object of its study from theology.[6] The Church historian is different from the theologian, not because he can do without theology, but because this is not the field in which he develops his knowledge. The historian needs some theological knowledge in order to understand the human events that are centered on the Church, just as the theologian cannot do without all historical knowledge unless he wants to make his doctrine an abstract speculation that entirely bypasses reality. Their methods of investigation are different, however. Faith must always illuminate the steps of the Catholic historian, above all when the object of his investigation is the Church, but the method that he follows and the questions that he poses are not those of a theologian or of a pastor.

The claim to evaluate an historical work by criteria belonging to other disciplines is therefore not only an epistemological error but also, on the moral level, a rash judgment, resulting from an ideological *a priori* assumption. I intend to respond, as a preventive measure, to the possibility of these rash judgments, using the pages of the leading histories of the Church, whose authors have never failed to express their respectful criticisms with regard to popes, conclaves, Councils and ecclesial events of all sorts.

I will do this, in particular, by referring to two historians, chosen neither from among the oldest nor from among the most modern, but rather from among the most reliable, because their works were highly praised by popes such as Leo XIII and St. Pius X: I am referring to the *Handbook of General Church History*[7] by Cardinal Josef

---

[6] Hubert Jedin, *Introduzione alla storia della Chiesa*, Italian translation (Brescia: Morcelliana, 1973), 42.

[7] Joseph Hergenröther, *Handbuch der allgemeinen Kirchengeschichte*, 3 vols. (Freiburg im Breisgau: Herder, 1876-1880), 4th edition by Peter Kirsch (1902).

Hergenröther[8] and to the *History of the Popes from the Close of the Middle Ages*[9] by Baron Ludwig von Pastor.[10]

Hergenröther's work extends from the birth of the Church to the pontificate of Leo XIII; Pastor's covers the period from the beginning of the Avignon Exile of the popes, in 1305, to the election of Pius VII to the pontificate on March 14, 1800. Both are conducted with a rigorous historical method and are animated by a deep love for the Church and her institutions.

Indeed, anyone who had time to browse through these works would realize that their authors do not hide any dark page of Church history, convinced as they are that her grandeur and divine character come to the fore precisely in those dark hours. Cardinal Hergenröther was convinced that "the best defense of the popes is to reveal what they were,"[11] and what is expected of the historian "is the objectively faithful and altogether dispassionate exposition of the facts that he has sincerely examined; in all else he must be free to engrave for us as it were the imprint of his religious principles."[12] As

---

[8] Joseph Hergenröther was born in Würzburg on September 15, 1824, and died in the Cistercian monastery of Mehrerau (Bregenz, Austria) on October 3, 1890. After studying in Rome and Munich, he was professor of Church history and Canon Law in Würzburg. Pius IX invited him to Rome in 1867 to serve as consultor in the preparation of Vatican Council I, and Leo XIII, in recognition of his accomplishments, created him cardinal in 1879, appointing him Prefect of the Papal Archive, an institution that he managed to open up to all scholars. His *magnum opus* is the *Handbuch der allgemeinen Kirchengeschichte*, written after Vatican Council I and expanded several times until the above-cited edition edited by J. P. Kirsch, who then added a supplement and an index, tracing the facts down to the election of Pius XI (1923). See the article about him by Celestino Testore in EC, 6:1415-1416.

[9] Ludwig von Pastor, *History of the Popes from the Close of the Middle Ages*, 26 vols. (St. Louis: Herder, 1898-); reprinted in 40 vols. (Wilmington, NC: Consortium, 1978-).

[10] Baron Ludwig von Pastor, born in Aachen on January 31, 1854, died in Innsbruck on September 30, 1928, taught history at the University of Innsbruck (1881-1900), was director of the Institute of Austrian History in Rome (1901-1915 and 1921-1928) and plenipotentiary minister of Austria to the Holy See (1921-1928). In 1886 the first volume of his *Geschichte der Päpste seit dem Ausgang des Mittelalters* appeared in print, which consists of 16 books in 22 volumes. Citations are taken from the Consortium edition. See the article about him by Francesco Cognasso in EC, 9:925-928.

[11] Cf. Giacomo Martina, "L'apertura dell'Archivio Vaticano: il significato di un centenario," in *Archivum Historiae Pontificiae* 19 (1981): 260.

[12] Hergenröther, 1:8.

for Baron von Pastor, Monsignor Pio Cenci, who edited the Italian edition of the work, relates that the German historian, when asked one day about his method, which consisted of prominently setting out the shadows and highlights of the pontificates that he treated, answered with these words: "There is nothing to fear: I have said everything, but I said it as a son compelled to reveal the faults of a most beloved Mother."[13]

Leo XIII, a pope who was a great promoter of historical as well as philosophical and theological studies, says that the history of the Church is like a mirror in which her life through the centuries shines.

> They who study it must never lose sight of the fact that it contains a body of dogmatic facts which none may call in question.... Still, inasmuch as the Church, which continues among men the life of the Word Incarnate, is composed of a divine and human element, this latter must be expounded by teachers and studied by disciples with great probity. "God has no need of our lies," as we are told in the Book of Job (13:7).
>
> The Church historian will be all the better equipped to bring out her divine origin, superior as this is to all conceptions of a merely terrestrial and natural order, the more loyal he is in extenuating nothing of the trials which the faults of her children, and at times even of her ministers, have brought upon the Spouse of Christ during the course of centuries. Studied in this way, the history of the Church constitutes by itself a magnificent and conclusive demonstration of the truth and divinity of Christianity.[14]

The Church, in her human component, can commit errors, and these errors, these sufferings, according to Leo XIII, can be caused by her sons and even by her ministers. But this takes nothing away from the grandeur and indefectibility of the Mystical Body of Christ. Holiness is an irremovable mark of the Church, but it does not mean the impeccability of her pastors, not even of the Supreme Pastors,

---

[13] Mons. Pio Cenci, "Cenni biografici del barone Ludwig von Pastor," in Ludwig von Pastor, *Storia dei Papi dalla fine del Medioevo* (Rome: Desclée & C., 1926-1963), 1:xxiii.

[14] Leo XIII, Encyclical *Depuis le jour* to the bishops of France on the education of the clergy (September 8, 1899), in *ASS* 32 (1899): 193-219; English text at https://w2.vatican.va/content/leo-xiii/en/encyclicals/documents/hf_l-xiii_enc_08091899_depuis-le-jour.html. Pope Leo's program for historical research is contained in the letter *Saepenumero considerantes* (August 18, 1883) in *ASS* 16 (1883-1884): 49-57, which was sent to Cardinals Antonino de Luca, Giovanni Battista Pitra and Joseph Hergenröther.

with regard to not only their personal life but also the higher *munus* [office] entrusted to them: the exercise of government. The infallibility of the Church's Magisterium does not mean that it has not experienced schisms and heresies over the course of her history that have painfully divided the successors of the apostles and, in some cases, grazed the Chair of Peter itself.

A Catholic historian can therefore freely reconstruct events and formulate judgments on the actions of the ecclesiastical authorities, provided that he strives always to seek the truth and is motivated by the love of the Church and not by the desire to denigrate her. If historical facts pose theological problems, the historian cannot ignore them and must bring them to light, referring always to the doctrine of the Church. In the same way, on the theological level, all baptized persons have the right to bring up problems and to pose questions to the legitimate ecclesiastical authorities, even though no one has the authority to replace the supreme Magisterium of the Church in order to resolve the disputed points definitively.

Before they are historians or theologians, Catholic scholars are members of the Mystical Body of Christ and have not only the right but the duty to study, with the competence that is proper to them, all the questions of faith and morals of which the Church, and she alone, is the guardian and teacher. Every Catholic, whatever his position and his role in the Church and in civil society may be, has the right to raise questions and to call upon ecclesiastical authority to resolve them, through the supreme word of its Magisterium. This is what I propose to do in the second part of this study, which is dedicated to establishing what the Church's rule of faith is in times of crisis like the one in which we are living.

Formerly, besides catechisms, invaluable manuals of theology for lay people were composed for the purpose of inviting the faithful, not to pursue theology, but rather to know good theology and, through it, to love the faith of the Church.[15] As a simple believer, I do not intend in the following pages to strike the pose of a theologian, but much more simply to recall some doctrinal benchmarks that ought to be known by every Catholic with an average education,

---

[15] See, for example, the *Dizionario di teologia dommatica per laici* by Monsignors Pietro Parente (later a cardinal) and Antonio Piolanti (Rome: Studium, 1943), which is still an effective guide.

and on this basis to invite the reader to make a reflection. My points of reference are the most trustworthy theologians of the Scholastic era, the Counter-Reformation and of the Roman school of the 19th and 20th centuries, which are still flourishing; furthermore, naturally and primarily, I will reference the Magisterium of the Supreme Pontiffs, up to the present one. If anyone disagrees, let him refute these doctrines, which I am simply repeating; this position is not mine but that of Tradition; I merely expound it at the level of historical facts and theological principles, submitting it to the final judgment of ecclesiastical authority.

Splendore Veritatis gaudet Ecclesia.[16] The Church, Leo XIII said, does not fear the truth.[17] There is only one truth, who is Jesus Christ, the Son of God and God Himself, Founder and Head of the Mystical Body that is the Church. The truth of the Church and about the Church is the truth of Christ and about Christ, in the encounter with Him who yesterday, today and always is presented to us as the unique "Way, Truth and Life" (Jn. 14:6).

---

[16] "The Church rejoices in the splendor of truth." Address (May 4, 1902) to representatives of the Institutes of Foreign History in Rome, quoted by Cardinal Raffaele Farina in "Leone XIII e la Biblioteca Apostolica Vaticana," in *Leone XIII e gli studi storici*, Atti del Congresso internazionale commemorativo (Città del Vaticano, 30-31 ottobre 2003), ed. Cosimo Semeraro (Vatican City, Libreria Editrice Vaticana, 2004), 107.

[17] Arnold Esch, "Leone XIII: L'apertura dell'Archivio Segreto Vaticano e la storiografia," in *Leone XIII e gli studi storici, op. cit.*, 31.

Apologia for Tradition

I

The Church Militant in the Most Difficult Hours of Its History

1. The era of persecutions

The history of the Church, over the course of two millennia, has never been peaceful and tranquil. She has always experienced external persecutions and internal crises and has always confronted them with a militant spirit. The first internal crisis occurred at the Council of Jerusalem in the year 50 A.D., in which the Apostle Paul "withstood" Peter, the head of the apostles, "to the face" (Gal. 2:11), reproaching his conduct toward the pagans. At that moment, as Romano Amerio remarks, the nascent Church, through this separation between the Synagogue and Christianity, rejected any form of syncretism between the Gospel and the Jewish Torah and affirmed her universal mission.[1]

Jesus Christ, Son of God, and Himself God, the founder and Head of the Catholic Church, entrusted to His disciples the mission of bringing the Gospel message not only to all individual human beings, but to all nations (Mt. 28:19; Rom. 1:5). This could have happened not in conflict but in collaboration with the temporal authorities of the world, because Jesus affirmed the distinction between the religious and the civil order, between Church and State. The Roman Empire, however, incited by the Sanhedrin, not only condemned Jesus to death but also with a Senate consultation, which all persecutors would then cite, denied legal status to Christianity and, under Nero, started the first bloody persecution against it.[2] The Empire, which made all sects equal in the Pantheon, denied Christianity the right to present itself as the absolute saving truth.

---

[1] Romano Amerio, *Iota Unum: A Study of Changes in the Catholic Church in the XXth Century*, translated by Rev. John P. Parsons (Kansas City, MO: Sarto House, 1996), 15.

[2] On this point see Marta Sordi, *I cristiani e l'Impero romano* (Milan: Jaca Book, 2004).

But Christians did not give up their public testimony to their Faith, recalling the words of the Gospel: "I send you as sheep in the midst of wolves" (Mt. 10:16) and "If any man will come after me, let him deny himself and take up his cross and follow me. For he that will save his life shall lose it" (Mt. 16:24-25).

The persecutions lasted, on and off, for three centuries. What had been condemned was not the Christians' behavior but their *nomen* [name], their very profession of Faith. During the harshest phases, anyone who declared himself a Christian was beheaded, crucified, burned, or fed to wild beasts in a stadium in front of a tumultuous crowd. And yet, during the first three centuries of the Church's life, thanks to an extraordinary assistance of grace, the apostles and their disciples brought the Christian message to Africa and India, to Britain and to the forests of Germany: from Jerusalem, as it says in Acts, "even to the uttermost part of the earth" (Acts 1:8). The blood of the martyrs, as Tertullian said, was the seed of Christians,[3] *quorum nomina Deus scit*, whose names only God knows, as the ancient documents would say. The Mystical Body of Christ experienced what its Head had experienced on Calvary.

The final and cruelest persecution, the work of Diocletian, raged between 295 and 305. Who could have imagined that, after a few years, a new young Emperor, Constantine, hoisting the standard of the Cross, would rout his enemy Maxentius at the gates of Rome and, a few months later in 313, with the Edict of Milan, would grant full freedom and legal rights to the Christian name? A radical turning point in history took its name from Constantine. Thanks to their new status, Christians abandoned the catacombs to occupy public places with their basilicas and ceremonies, with their own clergy and their own faithful.

And yet, at precisely that moment, Christianity found itself confronting one of the most terrible crises in its history. It was the collision with surviving paganism, which during the reign of Julian the Apostate attempted its final revenge. We mean above all the struggle against the first great internal enemy of the Church, Arianism.

---

[3] Tertullian, *Apologeticum*, 50 (PL 1, 534).

2. The Arian crisis in the fourth century

Arius, a priest in Alexandria, claimed that the Word, the Second Person of the Holy Trinity, was not equal to the Father but rather was created by Him, as a middle term between God and man, and hence had a substance different from the Father's divine substance. Constantine convoked in 325 in Nicaea the first major Ecumenical Council of the Church, at which, thanks to the decisive contribution of St. Athanasius,[4] Bishop of Alexandria, the doctrine of the "consubstantiality" of nature among the three Persons of the Holy Trinity was defined.

Not even ten years had passed since Nicaea when Arianism made deep inroads into the Church, so much so that two assemblies of bishops, in Caesarea and Tyre (334-335), condemned Athanasius for rebellion and fanaticism. The champion of the orthodox faith was deposed from his Episcopal see and was forbidden to set foot in Alexandria for the rest of his life. Between the uncompromising "party" of Athanasius and the Arian party, however, a "third party" made its way, that of the "semi-Arians," who in turn were divided into several sects: Anomoeans, Omoeans, and Homoousians, who acknowledged a certain analogy between the Father and the Son but denied that latter was "begotten, not made, consubstantial with the Father," as the Nicene Creed asserted. Athanasius was severely persecuted by his own brother bishops, and five times between 336 and 366 he was forced to abandon the city of which he was bishop, spending long years of exile and strenuous battles in defense of the Faith. In 341, while a Council of 50 bishops in Rome proclaimed Athanasius innocent, the great Council of the Dedication in Antioch, attended by more than 90 bishops, ratified the acts of the Synods of Caesarea and Tyre and set an Arian on the episcopal throne of Athanasius. That council's formulas of faith, according to Cardinal Hergenröther, "contained nothing heretical, but neither did they proclaim the whole Catholic truth in its entirety."[5]

The following Council of Sardica in 343 ended with a schism: the Western Fathers declared the deposition of Athanasius illegal and reconfirmed the Council of Nicaea; the Eastern Fathers, who held separate sessions, condemned not only Athanasius, but also

---

[4] See the extensive article by X. Le Bachelet in DTC, I, 2, cols. 2143-2176.
[5] Hergenröther, 2:56.

the pope, St. Julius I (337-352) who had supported him. Constans, the only ruler of the Empire after the death of his brothers, under the influence of his semi-Arian counselors, convened a series of new synods to destroy the "heresy" of the supporters of the Council of Nicaea. The Council of Sirmium in 351 sought a middle way between Catholic orthodoxy and Arianism.[6] At the Council of Arles in 353, the Fathers, including the legate from Liberius (352-366),[7] who had succeeded Julius I as pope, signed the condemnation of Athanasius. St. Paulinus, Bishop of Trier, was almost the only one who fought for the Nicene Faith and was exiled to Phrygia, where he died as a result of the mistreatment that he endured at the hands of the Arians.[8] Two years later, at the Council of Milan (355), more than 300 bishops from the West signed the condemnation of Athanasius, and another orthodox Father of the Church, St. Hilary of Poitiers, was banished to Phrygia for his uncompromising fidelity to orthodoxy. In 357 Pope Liberius, overcome by the sufferings of exile and by the insistence of his friends, but also spurred by "love of peace," signed the semi-Arian formula of Sirmium[9] and broke off communion with St. Athanasius, declaring him separated from the Roman Church because of his use of the term "consubstantial," that are testified by four letters transmitted to us by St. Hilary.[10] During the pontificate of that same Liberius, the Councils of Rimini (359) and Seleucia (359), which made up one great Council representing West and East, abandoned the term "consubstantial" of Nicaea and established an ambiguous "middle way" between the Arians and St. Athanasius. It seemed that the spreading heresy had been victorious in the Church.

St. Robert Bellarmine did not consider Liberius a heretic, although he admitted that he had sinned in his outward comport-

---

[6] *Ibid.*, 2:62.
[7] *Ibid.*, 2:68. *Cf.* also Vincenzo Monachino, S.J., "Il primato nella controversia ariana," in: *Saggi storici intorno al Papato* (Rome: Pontificia Università Gregoriana, 1959), 17-90 at 50-51.
[8] Hergenröther, 2:63.
[9] *Ibid.*, 2:68.
[10] Manlio Simonetti, *La crisi ariana del IV secolo* (Rome: Institutum Patristicum Augustinianum, 1975), 235-236. There is no reason to doubt the authenticity of the four letters, Simonetti remarks (see also his article "Liberio" in EP, 1:343), especially since other sources confirm that Liberius yielded (St. Athanasius, *Apologia contra Arianos*, 89; *Historia arianorum*, 41; St. Jerome, *De viris illustribus*, 97).

ment by favoring heresy.[11] The twin Councils of Seleucia and Rimini, convoked by the Emperor and intended to be ecumenical, like the Council of Nicaea (325), are not numbered among the eight Ecumenical Councils of antiquity by the Church today. They nevertheless had as many as 560 bishops in attendance, almost all the Fathers of Christianity, and they appeared "ecumenical" to their contemporaries. "The persecutors of the Church," Hergenröther writes, "were no longer external enemies, but her followers, her sons. The official appearance contrasted in every respect with the reality."[12] That was when St. Jerome coined the expression: "The whole world groaned and was astonished to find itself Arian."[13] And yet the Church continued to be not only *una et sancta* [one and holy], but *catholica*, that is, universal, because her message remained universal and capable of reaching all human beings and all nations, even when they strayed from it, as it happened during the Arian crisis.

Only the Council of Constantinople, convoked by the Emperor Theodosius the Great in 381, during the reign of Pope St. Damasus (367-384) signaled the end of Arianism in the Empire. It defined that the Holy Ghost is truly God, like the Son and the Father. While he had not convoked the Council, Damasus confirmed its canons, except for the third one, because it was detrimental to the rights of the Church of Rome.[14] The Council of Constantinople was then recognized as the second of the Ecumenical Councils.

Thanks to the Emperor Theodosius, Christianity was declared the State religion, and now it could be said that the work begun with Constantine's victory at Saxa Rubra on October 28, 312, was truly completed.

---

[11] St. Robert Bellarmine, *De Romano Pontifice*, Lib. IV, cap. IX, in: *De controversiis christianae fidei* (Venice: Apud Societatem Minimam, 1599) 1:814.

[12] Hergenröther, 2:73.

[13] St. Jerome, *Dialogus adversus Luciferianos*, 19 in PL 23, 171. "*Ingemuit totus orbis, et Arianum se esse miratus est*," and he adds: "*Periclitabatur navicula Apostolorum, urgebant venti, fluctibus latera tundebantur: nihil jam supererat spei: Dominus excitatur, imperat tempestati, bestia (scil. Constantius) moritur, tranquillitas rediit*" (*ibid.*, cols. 172-173.) "The ship of the apostles was in peril, she was driven by the wind, her sides beaten with the waves: no hope was now left. But the Lord awoke and made the tempest cease; the beast [Constans] died, and there was a calm once again" (NPNF-2 6:329b).

[14] According to Canon 3 of the Council of Constantinople, "the Bishop of Constantinople will have the primacy of honor after the Bishop of Rome, because that city is the New Rome" (COE, p. 32).

St. Ambrose had formulated the sacrosanct principle *Ubi Petrus ibi Ecclesia* [Where Peter is, there is the Church], but anyone who had tried to follow that principle literally in that era would have followed the error of Liberius and abandoned orthodoxy. "Peter" is the unchangeable institution, not the man who can make mistakes. Within the 60 years between the Council of Nicaea and the Council of Constantinople, the living Magisterium of the Church stopped reaffirming Catholic truth clearly, yet without ever falling into formal heresy. Did the Holy Ghost therefore stop assisting the Church? No, because the Faith was kept by a minority of saints and indomitable bishops, like Athanasius of Alexandria, Hilary of Poitiers, Eusebius of Vercelli, and above all by the faithful people, who did not go along with the theological diatribes but preserved the right doctrine simply by their *sensus fidei*.

In 1859 John Henry Newman, who had already been a Catholic for 14 years, wrote in an article that during the Arian crisis the *Ecclesia docens* [teaching Church] had not proved in all circumstances to be the active instrument of the infallible Church.[15] The young Fr. (later Cardinal) Giovanni Battista Franzelin objected that this statement seemed prejudicial to the indefectibility of the Church. Cardinal Newman—today a Blessed—explained his thinking in these terms on the occasion of the third edition of *Arians of the Fourth Century*, in 1871:

> I mean still, that in that time of immense confusion the divine dogma of our Lord's divinity was proclaimed, enforced, maintained, and (humanly speaking) preserved, far more by the "*Ecclesia docta*" ["instructed Church"] than by the "*Ecclesia docens*" ["teaching Church"]; that the body of the Episcopate was unfaithful to its commission, while the body of the laity was faithful to its baptism; that at one time the pope, at other times a patriarchal, metropolitan, or other great see, at other times general councils, said what they should not have said, or did what obscured and compromised revealed truth; while, on the other hand, it was the Christian people, who, under Providence, were the ecclesiastical strength of Athana-

---

[15] *Cf.* John Henry Newman, *On Consulting the Faithful in Matters of Doctrine* (July 1859).

sius, Hilary, Eusebius of Vercelli, and other great solitary confessors, who would have failed without them...[16]

The controversy had caused a sensation. But the fact that in 1879 Leo XIII elevated Newman to the cardinalatial purple was a ringing confirmation of the orthodoxy of his words which, far from criticizing infallibility, only served to confirm it. There is a *sensus fidei* that embrace the whole living and lived Faith of the Church, which is made up of a teaching part (*docens*) and a part that is instructed or learning (*discens*). Teaching revealed truth infallibly is the responsibility of the *teaching* Church alone, while the *learning* Church receives and preserves this truth. But, as theologians teach, besides the infallibility in teaching there is also an infallibility in believing. Obviously the judgment of an individual believer is not infallible: but the faithful as a whole cannot err in their belief. Indeed, if the flock of believers, as a whole, could err, believing as Revelation something that is not such, this would frustrate the promise of divine assistance to the Church. What good would it be to proclaim a dogma that was believed only by the one, the Roman Pontiff, who proclaimed it? In the 60 years of the Arian crisis, there was no infallible pronouncement of the teaching Church, which often appeared uncertain and lost, but the *sensus fidelium* [sense of the faithful] preserved the integrity of the Faith.

In the course of the Arian crisis the Christian people showed an attachment to the orthodox Faith that was purer than that of their own pastors; this was also because they did not understand the subtleties of the heretics. St. Hilary of Poitiers in his *Contra Auxen-*

---

[16] *Cf.* John Henry Newman, *Arians of the Fourth Century* (London: Longmans, Green & Co., 18907), 465-466. The passage is part of the essay "The Orthodoxy of the Body of the faithful during the Supremacy of Arianism" (Appendix, pp. 445-468), which corrects the controversial article that had appeared in *The Rambler* in 1859. Newman explains also that he himself wrote as an historian and that "while it is historically true, it is in no sense doctrinally false, that a pope, as a private doctor, and much more bishops, when not teaching formally, may err, as we find they did err in the 4th century" (p. 464). Against his critics he repeats that in the 60 years that passed between the Council of Nicaea (325) and the Council of Constantinople (381) there was a temporary uncertainty ("suspense") of the functions of the *Ecclesia docens*, by which he means that in this period there was no authoritative pronouncement of the infallible voice of the Church and "there was nothing, after Nicaea, of firm, unvarying, consistent testimony, for nearly 60 years" (*ibid.*, p. 466).

tium[17] writes that the Arians in their preaching to the people said the same things as the Catholics, nevertheless in their mind they made qualifications and exceptions, so that they thought in one way and preached in another, and he concludes: "*Sanctiores aures plebis quam corda sacerdotum*"—"The ears of the people are more sacred than the hearts of the priests."[18] St. Athanasius declares the same thing: "In every church the faithful preserve the Faith that they have learned, look for their own teachers, condemn the heresy that is contrary to Christ, and flee all its defenders like a snake."[19]

After recalling the remark by St. Paulinus of Nola, "*Ab omnium fidelium ore pendeamus, quia in omnem fidelem Spiritus Sanctus spirat*"—"We hang on the lips of all the faithful, because the Holy Spirit breathes in every believer," the eminent theologian Matthias Scheeben comments:

> Certainly this *sensus fidelium* is as a rule at the same time the effect and the echo of the present teaching or else of the preceding explicit and consistent teaching of the Magisterium; but from this it follows only that it is also at the same time a sign and proof for the presence of the actual doctrinal tradition. It can therefore still be of great importance, when its unity and firmness are for the moment somewhat more evident than the teaching of the whole Magisterium, or when a part of the Magisterium, as in the time of Arianism (when St. Hilary could say [*Contra Auxentium*, 6]: "the faithful ears of the people are holier than the lips of the priests"), becomes unfaithful to Tradition, or when the Magisterium, for the purpose of solemnly defining a doctrine that temporarily had been disputed, wishes to seek support from all available manifestations of the Spirit of God in the Church (as in the case of the definition of the Immaculate Conception of Mary).[20]

3. Shadows and highlights of the first Councils

While the barbarians were invading the territory of the Empire, Arianism was followed by new, devastating schisms and heresies. Donatism, the first ecclesiological schism and then a heresy, taught that there is an invisible Church of the pure and the holy, as opposed

---

[17] St. Hilary of Poitiers, *Contra Arianos, vel Auxentium*, 6 (PL 10, 612 ff.).
[18] *Ibid.*, PL 10, 613.
[19] St. Athanasius, *Historia arianorum ad monachos*, 41, 9 (PG 25, 743).
[20] Matthias Joseph Scheeben, *Handbook of Catholic Dogmatics* (Steubenville: Emmaus Academic Press, 2018), vol. 1.1, no. 325.

to the institutional Church and her sacraments. Pelagianism claimed that salvation is possible by human efforts, thus frustrating the decisive role of divine grace. Manichaeism asserted the existence of a principle of evil that was ontologically opposed to the principle of good. All these heresies were opposed with extraordinary vigor by a Berber of Roman extraction, Augustine, who would go down in history together with the name of the city of which he was the bishop for 30 years, Hippo. It is said that the Vandals waiting for his death to conquer that city and then Carthage, overwhelming Christian Africa even before Islam. St. Augustine's masterpiece, *The City of God*, originated as a meditation on the fall of Rome, which had been invaded by Alaric's Visigoths in 410. The African bishops—and besides Augustine we should also recall the names of Cyprian and Aurelius—distinguished themselves by their fidelity to the Church of Rome in an era when the Faith seemed to vacillate in Rome itself.

The heresy of Pelagius implied the essential destruction of the whole supernatural order. Two Councils of African bishops, assembled in Carthage and Mileve, in 416, condemned the doctrines of Pelagius, asking Rome to reiterate its condemnation of the heretic. Pope Zosimus (417-418), elected to the papal throne in 417, declared instead, in the presence of the Roman clergy, the perfect orthodoxy of Pelagius, indignant that such a worthy man could be calumniated in that way.[21] Zosimus then sent two letters to the African bishops who had excommunicated Pelagius and his disciple Celestius, rebuking the frivolity they had displayed in condemning the two heretics. The African bishops, assembled in Carthage, for their part accused Pope Zosimus of promoting the Pelagian heresy. They were right, Cardinal Hergenröther admits, and he censures the conduct of Pope Zosimus, while stating that although he "lacked foresight…he did not err in the Faith."[22] Five bishops, among them St. Augustine, appealed to the new pope, St. Boniface I (418-423), who, changing the line of

---

[21] Letter *Postquam nobis*, dated September 21, 417, in Mansi, vol. IV, col. 353. No doubt it was in that winter of 417-418, Georges de Plinval comments ("Le lotte del pelagianesimo," in: P. de Labriolle, G. Bardy, L. Brehier, and G. de Plinval, *Storia della Chiesa*, vol. IV [Turin: S.A.I.E., 1961], 131-132), that St. Augustine spent the most anguished hours of his episcopal career, feeling that he had been disowned by the See of Peter, and he addressed to Rome an energetic *obtestatio* (not "obstestatio") [entreaty] (St. Augustine, *Contra duas epistolas Pelag.*, II, 5). On Zosimus and the Pelagian question, *cf.* E. Amann, DTC, XV 2, cols. 3708-3716.

[22] Hergenröther, 2:271.

his predecessor, condemned Pelagius and Celestius. That was when St. Augustine wrote the famous line: "the case is closed."[23]

During those same years, in the East, a new heresiarch, Nestorius, denied the substantial unity of the Person of Christ and Mary's divine motherhood. When he disputed the Christian people's right to call the Virgin Mary the Mother of God, the Patriarch remained silent, and a simple layman, Eusebius, who would later become the Bishop of Dorylaeum, was the one to rebel publicly against him, defending Catholic Tradition.[24] Lay people personally participated in the battles in defense of the Faith from the 4th to the 5th century. Theologians explain how "under the inspiration of the Holy Ghost, the faithful can be prompted to understand and to believe better when their piety and worship increase, thus promoting the progress of dogma. Indeed, the murmuring of the faithful against Nestorius was of great help in defining the divine Motherhood of the Blessed Virgin..."[25]

At the Council of Ephesus, held in 431, the defenders of orthodoxy, led by Cyril, Patriarch of Alexandria, confronted the proponents of heterodoxy, headed by Nestorius, who had become Patriarch of Constantinople. After some back-and-forth, orthodoxy triumphed and Mary was solemnly proclaimed *Theotokos*, "God-bearer," Mother of God. The definition of the dogma of Mary's divine motherhood was enthusiastically greeted by the people who were anxiously waiting, so much so that "there was but little sleep in Ephesus that night; for very joy they remained awake."[26] So it happened, Cardinal Newman recalls, with the doctrine of the Real Presence of Christ in the Eucharist, when "Paschasius was supported by the faithful in his maintenance of it... [against] the learned Benedictines of Germany and France."[27]

Already in that tempestuous era it was clearly evident that holiness of life is always accompanied by purity of doctrine. This is the reason why, since that time, as the Servant of God Dom Guéranger

---

[23] *Ibid.*, 2:270. This remark by St. Augustine (in *Sermo* 131, 10, 10) is the basis of the axiom, "*Roma locuta est, causa finita*"—"Rome has spoken, the case is closed."
[24] *Ibid.*, 2:230.
[25] Jean-Maria Hervé, *Manuale Theologiae Dogmaticae* (Paris: Berche et Pagis, 1953), 3:305.
[26] John Henry Newman, *On Consulting the Faithful in Matters of Doctrine*.
[27] *Ibid.*

writes, the Church has been saved by the saints: "Just as St. Athanasius was elected to combat the Arians and St. Augustine—to dispute the Pelagians, so too St. Cyril was raised up by God to oppose Nestorius victoriously." Dom Guéranger celebrates that saint by writing:

> When the shepherd turns into a wolf, it is up to the flock especially to defend itself. As a rule, no doubt, doctrine comes down from the bishops to the faithful; and in the field of Faith the subordinates must not judge the leaders. But in the treasury of revelation there are essential points of which every Christian, by the very fact that he is Christian, must have the necessary knowledge and the due custody.[28]

The name of Cyril, the great opponent of Nestorius, was invoked to justify a contrary heresy, that of the Archimandrite Eutychus. He and his followers maintained that the human nature in Christ had been absorbed by the divine nature and that therefore we must speak not only about one Person but also about one nature. Once again it was Eusebius who, in November 448, stood up in the assembly of bishops gathered in Constantinople to indict publicly the heresy of Eutychus, who was protected by the Patriarch of Constantinople, Flavianus.[29] But the Emperor Theodosius II, under pressure from the Patriarch of Alexandria, Dioscuros, convoked a Council in Ephesus to rehabilitate Eutychus. The pope, St. Leo the Great, was denied the presidency of the Council, and he branded the assembly of bishops with the famous title of *Latrocinium*, or Robbers' Council of Ephesus. Leo requested a new Council, and finally the successor of Theodosius, Marcian, urged also by his energetic, orthodox wife Pulcheria, convened the Fourth Ecumenical Council in Chalcedon. There the primacy of the Bishop of Rome was newly and solemnly acknowledged, and the heresies of Nestorius and Eutychus were once again condemned.[30]

Bishops, doctors, monks, and consecrated virgins were the only restraining wall against the barbarians who had overthrown the Roman legions; not only that, but they were also the bulwark of the Faith in a time when so many pastors defected. And the sins of the West, according to St. Jerome, should be regarded as the main reason for the barbarian invasions. "It is a disgrace for us," he exclaimed,

---

[28] *Cf.* Dom Prosper Guéranger, *Année liturgique* (Tours: Mame, 192), 15th ed., 340-341.
[29] Hergenröther, 2:246-247.
[30] DH 300-303.

"who make ourselves so little acceptable to God. His wrath strikes us through the barbarians' violence."[31]

The 6th century was, in certain respects, even worse than the previous one. The Roman Empire had vanished; chaos seemed to reign in society. In Africa, now freed from the Vandals, the bishops continued to defend their Faith against the Emperors, from Justinian to Heraclius, but they did not always have the support of Rome. The Emperor Justinian, in order to impose religious peace, sought in his imperial edict of the "Three Chapters"[32] to impose a compromise between the orthodox Catholics and the Monophysites. Pope Vigilius (537-555) subscribed to the imperial act with a *judicatum*. The Fifth Ecumenical Council, Constantinople II, convoked in 553 by the Emperor Justinian, was rather badly received by the orthodox bishops of the West. Pope Vigilius refused to participate in it, and Eutychus, Patriarch of Constantinople, presided at it. The Emperor, who had convoked and imposed it, persecuted the opponents of the Council, among them St. Paulinus of Aquileia. Only with the passage of time did this Synod, with a heretic presiding, acquire the title of "Ecumenical."[33]

In the complex theological controversy, Pope Vigilius[34] was accused by the defenders of the orthodox Faith, such as Bishop Facundus of Hermiana,[35] of having adopted the heretical thesis of Monophysitism, and therefore the African bishops went so far as to excommunicate him. When he died, his corpse was not entombed in St. Peter's Basilica, as a sign of *damnatio memoriae* ["accursed memory"]. The attitude of Vigilius, too, and of his successor Pelagius, like that of Liberius and Zosimus, was judged ambiguous by Church historians and by their contemporaries.

Nevertheless, during that same period, the Primacy of the Church of Rome was asserted more and more forcefully. To St. Leo (440-461), the first pope to whom posterity attributed the title of

---

[31] Cited in Massimiliano Ghilardi and Luca Pilara, *I barbari che presero Roma: Il sacco del 410 e le sue conseguenze* (Rome: Acqua Pia Antica Marcia, 2010), 111.

[32] *Cf.* the articles by E. Amann, in DTC, XV, 2, cols. 1868-1924, and Cardinal Agostino Mayer, in EC, XII, cols. 456-460.

[33] Hergenröther, 2:355.

[34] *Cf.* the article by Claire Sotinel, in EP, I, 512-529; E. Amann, DTC, "Trois chapîtres," XV, 2, cols. 1868-1924.

[35] Facundus of Hermiana, *Epistula Fidei Catholica in defensione trium capitulum*, in PL 67, 527-578.

"the Great," we owe the fullest theology of the papacy in the first millennium,[36] with the crucial distinction between the office and the one who holds it, between the public persona of the pope and his private person.[37] After the excommunication of the Patriarch of Constantinople, Acacius, by Pope Gelasius, Pope Hormisdas (514-523) in 517 made the Eastern bishops sign a profession of Faith in which they acknowledged their submission to the See of Peter.[38] On March 16, 536, the Emperor Justinian and the peoples of the East and West solemnly recognized the Primacy of the Chair of Peter. The following Ecumenical Councils approved this rule, which was constantly repeated if not always observed. From then on the Primacy of the Roman Pontiff has been accompanied inseparably by the Primacy of Sacred Tradition, as the "*regula fidei*" ["rule of faith"] of which the Bishop of Rome represented the supreme guarantee.

At least two Councils called the Roman Primacy into doubt: the Second Ecumenical Council of Constantinople described Constantinople as the "New Rome" and, while acknowledging the Primacy, questioned its divine origin; the Council of Chalcedon, in its Canon 28, repeated this error. That was the start of the dissension between the Church of Rome and the Churches of the East. Nevertheless, between the 5th and the 6th century the Catholic Church, devastated in Italy by the Gothic wars, torn in the East by the schismatic attitude of the Greeks, persecuted in Africa by the Vandals and in Armenia by the Persians, gave life in Gaul to the first European nation, the France of Clodovicus (Clovis).

4. "*Error cui non resistitur approbatur*"

At the beginning of the 7th century St. Gregory the Great (590-604) raised the banner of the papacy, while a legion of Benedictine monks launched a campaign to conquer the world. The grafting of Christianity onto *Romanità* produced splendid fruits. But the glorious names of Gregory and of many of his successors cannot make us forget the case of Pope Honorius (625-638), who in 634 approved the compromise between Catholic orthodox belief and Monophysitism

---

[36] *Cf.* Monsignor Roland Minnerath, *Le Pape évêque universel ou premier des évêques?* (Paris: Beauchesne, 1978).
[37] St. Leo the Great, *Epistula* 103, in PL 54, 292.
[38] DH 363-365.

contrived by Patriarch Sergius of Constantinople: Christ, according to this new heresy, called Monothelitism, supposedly had only one will, while having two natures. When Cyrus, the Patriarch of Alexandria, subscribed to the doctrine of the Patriarch of Constantinople, the heresy seemed to triumph.

The most renowned adversary of Monothelitism was St. Sophronius, Patriarch of Jerusalem beginning in year 634. Pope Honorius, Bishop of Rome, when called to adjudicate, sided however with the heretic Sergius against Sophronius and backed Monothelitism, so that the Emperor Heraclius published a doctrinal formula called *Ecthesis* (638) in which he imposed the new theology of the one will. In Rome, Pope St. Martin I (649-653), in a Council at the Lateran (649) in which St. Maximus the Confessor also took part, condemned the heresy of the Monothelites, but he was beaten and, along with St. Maximus, exiled from the Eternal City; while he was still alive, they elected his successor, Eugene I (654-657). This Council was not ecumenical, but it is very important because of the significance that was attributed to Tradition during it. It proclaims:

> If anyone does not, following the holy Fathers, confess properly and truly, in word and mind, even to the last point, all that has been handed down and proclaimed to the holy, Catholic, and apostolic Church of God by the holy Fathers and by the five venerable universal Councils, let him be condemned.[39]

The Third Council of Constantinople (November 2, 680 – September 16, 681), was called the Trullan Synod because the sessions, with the papal legates presiding, took place in the great hall with a cupola (*trullus*) in the imperial palace, reiterated the existence of the two wills, human and divine, in Christ, and declared anathema the memory of Honorius because he had accepted the "impious doctrine of Sergius."[40] The doctrinal acts, signed by 174 Council Fathers and by the Emperor, were sent to Pope Leo II (682-683) who, after approving them, ordered that they should be translated into Latin and signed by all the bishops of the West. Leo II accepted the judgment of the Council that anathematized his predecessor as a heretic,[41] asserting that Honorius "did not purify this apostolic Church by the doctrine of the apostolic tradition,

---
[39] DH 517.
[40] DH 550-559.
[41] DH 561-563.

but rather attempted to subvert the immaculate Faith by profane treason."[42] Hergenröther added that one could apply to Honorius the words used by his predecessors in the case of Acacius: *"Error cui non resistitur approbatur, et veritas quae minime defensatur opprimitur."*[43] "An error that is not opposed must be considered approved, and a truth that is minimally defended is in reality denied and oppressed."

Today, many Church historians like Hergenröther, while admitting that Honorius favored Monothelitism, consider him not heretical but, like Popes Zosimus and Vigilius, "a promoter of heresy."[44] The problem, however, does not spring from the theological censure reserved for his conduct, but rather from the fact that one Pontiff was considered heretical by a subsequent Pontiff and by an Ecumenical Council united with him. If an Ecumenical Council is always infallible when, in union with the Roman Pontiff, it promulgates decrees in matters of faith or morals, we must conclude that Honorius was infallibly declared heretical by the Third Council of Constantinople, the acts of which were approved by Pope Leo II, and that therefore it is possible, as theologians from then on have admitted almost unanimously, that a pope may fall into heresy. In a speech addressed to the Eighth Ecumenical Council, Hadrian II (867-872) stated: "It is true that after his death Honorius was anathematized by the Eastern Churches; but we must not forget that he was accused of heresy, the only crime that makes resistance of inferiors to superiors legitimate, just like the rejection of their pernicious doctrine."[45]

The case of Honorius is one of the arguments discussed by St. Robert Bellarmine in *De Romano Pontefice* to prove the possibil-

---

[42] DH 563.
[43] Hergenröther, 2:86.
[44] *Ibid.*, 2:386
[45] Cited in Cardinal Louis Billot, *Tractatus de Ecclesia Christi, sive Continuatio theologiae de verbo incarnato: tomo 1.: De credibilitate ecclesiae et de intima eius constitutione* (Rome: Universitas Gregoriana, 1921), 1:611.

ity of a heretical pope.[46] He remarks that, even though Honorius was probably not a true heretic, the fact remains that the subsequent Pontiffs considered him one. St. Robert distances himself both from the Protestants, who allow that a pope and an Ecumenical Council might set forth formal heresies, and from those who maintain that this could never happen, like the 15th-century Dutch theologian Albert Pighius.[47] The opinion that St. Robert Bellarmine presents as the most certain is *"communissima"* [quite common] among theologians and is *"quodammodo in medio, Pontificem, sive haereticus esse possit, sive non, non posse ullo modo definire aliquid haereticum a tota Ecclesia credendum."*[48]

Henceforth in the course of the first millennium, the doctrine of the Primacy of the Roman Pontiff can be said to be clearly defined. Pope St. Nicholas I (858-867) in a famous letter to the Eastern Emperor Michael, written on September 28, 865, recapitulated in systematic form the doctrine of the Roman Primacy.[49] This is the letter in which we find the famous expression: *Prima Sedes non judicabitur a quoquam*,[50] which is mentioned by Gratian in his famous

---

[46] St. Robert Bellarmine, *De Romano Pontifice*, Lib. II, cap. XXX, col. 691. "*Ubi notandum est, quod etsi probabile sit Honorium non fuisse haereticum et Hadrianum II Papam, deceptum ex corruptis exemplaribus VI. Synodi, falso putasse Honorium fuisse haereticum: tamen non possumus negare, quin Hadrianus cum Romano Concilio, immo et tota Synodus VIII generalis senserit, in cause haeresis posse Romanum Pontificem indicari*" ["Here it should be noted that, although it is probable that Honorius was not heretical and that Pope Hadrian II, deceived by corrupt copies of the Sixth Synod, wrongly thought that Honorius was a heretic, nevertheless we cannot deny that Hadrian with the Roman Council, indeed the whole Eighth General Synod thought that a Roman Pontiff can be indicted in a case of heresy."] The case of Pope Honorius is treated more fully by St. Robert in *De Romano Pontifice*, Lib. IV, cap. XI (*De Honorio I*), cols. 822-829. See also Fernand Cabrol, O.S.B., "La question d'Honorius," in DAFC, II, cols. 514-519; Georg Kreuzer, *Die Honoriusfrage im Mittelalter und in der Neuzeit* (Stuttgart: Anton Hiersemann, 1975); Elena Zocca, "Onorio I e la tradizione occidentale," in: *Augustinianum* 27 (1986): 571-615.

[47] On this topic see the groundbreaking study by Arnaldo Xavier da Silveira, "Hypothèse théologique d'un pape hérétique," in: *La nouvelle Messe de Paul VI: qu'en penser?* (Chiré-en-Montreuil: Diffusion de la Pensée française, 1975), 214-334.

[48] "…as it were in the middle: a Pontiff, whether or not he may be heretical, can by no means define something heretical to be believed by the whole Church." St. Robert Bellarmine, *De Romano Pontifice*, Lib. IV, cap. II, col. 794.

[49] DH 638-642.

[50] "The first See will not be judged by anyone…," DH 638. This text is included in the Decree of Gratian, Dist. XXI, c. 7, *Nunc autem*.

Decree in these words: *"A nemine est judicandus, nisi deprehenditur a fide devius,"* ("He must not be judged by anyone, unless he is caught straying from the Faith").

This rule, *Prima sedes non judicabitur*, admits only one exception: the sin of heresy. The possibility of judging the pope if he makes himself guilty of heresy was, as the great canonical collections testify, an undisputed maxim of the Middle Ages.[51] But who can judge the pope if no one is superior to him? The medieval decretists explain that, by falling into an error contrary to the Faith, the pope ceases to be the head of the Church and excludes himself from the hierarchy, and therefore any Catholic, strictly speaking, can accuse him, according to the words of the Evangelist John: "He that doth not believe is already judged" (Jn. 3:18). The Church's sentence is nothing but the verification of a fact.[52] It is not a matter of deposing a pope, but rather of verifying that a pope has fallen from his office through the sin of heresy. Hence, among the cases of loss of pontifical authority, Catholic doctrine calmly admits the possibility of a heretical pope.[53] This possibility does not contradict the dogma of infallibility, because infallibility does not mean the inerrancy of the pope as an individual, but rather the inerrancy of the papal office as such. Divine Providence spared the Church the tragedy of a pope known to be heretical, but not the distress of popes who promoted heresy and in the exercise of their governance disgraced themselves with serious sins, proving to be unworthy Vicars of Christ, but without ever losing their office.

5. When the philosophy of the Gospel governed the States

The last two Eastern Councils were held in 787 in Nicaea, at the initiative of the Empress Irene, and in 869-870 in Constantinople, following an agreement between the Emperor Basil the Macedonian

---

[51] Victor Martin, "Comment s'est formée la doctrine de la supériorité du Concile sur le Pape," in: *Revue des Sciences Religieuses* 2 (1937): 121-143.

[52] *Ibid.*, 129.

[53] *Cf.* St. Robert Bellarmine, *De Romano Pontifice*, Lib. II, cap. XXX, cols. 690-694; see also Franciscus X. Wernz, S.J., and Petrus Vidal, S.J., *Jus Canonicum* (Rome: Gregoriana, 1943), 2nd ed., 517 ff.; E. Dublanchy, "Infaillibilité du Pape," in: DTC, VII, 2, col. 1714; Charles Journet, *L'Église du Verbe incarné* (Paris: Desclée de Brouwer, 1941), 1:625 ff. and 2:1063 ff.

and Pope Hadrian II. These Councils of Nicaea and Constantinople, the seventh and eighth in Church history, condemned respectively the heresy of iconoclasm and the heresy of Photius, who denied the Roman authority. In the Eighth Council of the Church, the fourth one to be held in Constantinople, the seven preceding Ecumenical Councils were approved, and 109 bishops signed the condemnation of Photius and all who had persisted in his schism, dipping their pen into the Sacred Chalice that contained the Precious Blood of Jesus,[54] as Pope St. Theodore (642-649) had already done when he had signed the condemnation of Patriarch Pyrrhus. The schismatic Eastern Churches, which traced their origin back to the rebellion of Photius and of the subsequent rebellion of the Patriarch Michael Cerularius (1053), recognize as ecumenical only the first seven Councils of the Church, excluding Constantinople IV.

On Christmas Eve of the year 800, Charlemagne was crowned Emperor in Rome by Pope St. Leo II (795-818). This event, which marks the advent of the Western Holy Roman Empire, is just as important in the history of the Church as the Edict of Constantine. It can be considered the birth of Christian civilization, the era in which, according to Leo XIII, "the philosophy of the Gospel governed the States."[55] And yet, starting with the end of Charlemagne's rule, what Cardinal Baronio described as the Church's *"saeculum obscurum"* ["Dark Age"] began. This was a long period of degradation that witnessed, between 882 and 1046, a succession of 45 popes and anti-popes, of whom 15 were deposed and 14 were assassinated, imprisoned, or exiled.

Cardinal Hergenröther describes as *"vituperosa"*[56] or reprehensible the conduct of Pope Stephen VI (or VII) (896-897), who unearthed the cadaver of his predecessor Formosus (891-896), placed it on the throne in full view of the assembled synod and staged a macabre trial against him, which concluded with the condemnation of the cadaver, from which the two fingers used to bless were cut off before it was thrown into the Tiber. Did the Holy Ghost fail to assist the Church in that period? Certainly not: during that dark age in which unwor-

---

[54] Cesare Baronio, *Annales ecclesiastici* (Venice: Sumptibus Basilii et Tivani, 1705-1712), anno 869, no. 39; Karl Joseph von Hefele, *Histoire des Conciles d'après les documents originaux* (Paris: Letouzey et Ané, 1907), IV/1:533.

[55] Leo XIII, Encyclical *Immortale Dei* (November 1, 1885), in: *AAS* 18 (1885): 169.

[56] Hergenröther, 3:248.

thy representatives ascended to the papal throne, the Holy Ghost assisted the Church just as He assisted it when, as Cardinal Hergenröther writes, "throughout the first half of the 10th century everything seemed as though toppled from its status; worldly corruption seemed to flood into the Church, and the discipline of the Church was destroyed."[57]

The Conclave in 1033 elected "the licentious young man who under the name of Benedict IX was to disgrace the Church for nine years (1033-1044)."[58] In 1044 a general popular rebellion broke out against Benedict IX, and Bishop Giovanni di Sabina was elected with the name Sylvester III (1045). Benedict again took power in Rome, but that same year, in 1045, he abdicated in return for compensation, in favor of Archpriest Giovanni Graziano, who took the name Gregory VI (1045-1046). Then he regretted his resignation and sought, with the help of his faction, to take back the papal throne. "Thus for a time there were three claimants to the papal dignity: Benedict IX, who had resigned, Sylvester III, who was undoubtedly illegitimate, and Gregory VI, who despite the irregularity committed in his promotion was acknowledged by the nobility and by the greater part of the Church as the one true pope."[59] We may wonder where the Holy Ghost was during that era in which "the state of things was wretched"[60] for the Church. The answer is that, during that same period, the spirit of love for God and for His Church developed in an extraordinary way in a monastery in Bourgogne, the Abbey of Cluny, which was destined to go down in history for its grandiose and lasting work of reform.

The first Abbot of Cluny, Berno, was succeeded by a series of holy abbots who spread his spirit throughout Christendom, transforming the men and the institutions of the Medieval era. The monastic reform of Cluny expanded rapidly in Italy, Spain, and England, eventually numbering 3,000 monasteries that were dependent on the "mother house" in Bourgogne. This work was joined by other saints such as Romuald, Giovanni Gualberto, William of Dijon, and

---

[57] *Ibid.*, 3:252.
[58] *Ibid.*, 3:272. Benedict IX was born Theophylactus III of the Counts of Tusculum.
[59] *Ibid.*, 3:273. Hergenröther considers Sylvester III an anti-pope, but today his name is listed as a legitimate pope in the *Annuario Pontificio* from January 20 to March 10, 1045.
[60] *Ibid.*

Peter Damian. While the papacy was going through the period of its greatest degradation (without its essence being tarnished, however), holiness wafted elsewhere around the Holy Roman Empire, with St. Matilda, wife of Henry I, St. Adelaide, wife of the Emperor Otto I, St. Henry II and his saintly wife Cunegonde. New nations converted, and the year 1,000 seemed to inaugurate an era of rejuvenation for Europe which, according to the well-known words of the monk Rodulfus Glaber, seemed to be clothed in a white mantle of churches.[61]

Even in the periods of spiritual and moral depression experienced by the Church in her history, the truth of Christ and His law remain unchangeable, and the way to ascend to holiness is the same. The Church continues to be holy in her dogmas, in her sacraments, and in the souls that the Holy Ghost fills with His grace. Two wounds desolated the Church in the 11th century: simony and the moral depravity of the clergy. Connected with simony was the granting of offices and ecclesiastical benefices by the secular authorities; the moral depravity had one of its most infamous manifestations in the "cancer of the sodomite contamination" which, as St. Peter Damian wrote, raged "like a bloodthirsty beast in Christ's sheepfold."[62] The spiritual resources necessary to emerge from the crisis were drawn from the holiness of the monasteries. The See of St. Peter was occupied, between 1057 and 1118, by five popes from Benedictine monasteries: Stephen IX (1057-1058), St. Gregory VII (1073-1085), Blessed Victor III (1086-1087), Blessed Urban II (1088-1099), and Paschal II (1099-1118). The pontificate of Gregory VII in particular offers the model of an authentic spiritual and moral reform of the Church, based on the fullness of authority of the Successor of Peter. From this Gregorian and Cluniac spirit of reform was born, to the cry of *"Deus vult"* ["God wills it!"], the epoch of the Crusades, a luminous page of Church history from the 11th to the 13th century.

Even in the following centuries, the popes were not impeccable—neither in their personal conduct nor in their exercise of governance—yet the Church continued to be holy and to sanctify souls. On April 5, 1058, when Bishop Giovanni Mincio of Velletri

---

[61] Rodulfus Glaber, *Historiarum sui temporis lib. III*, in PL 142, 651.

[62] St. Peter Damian, *Liber Gomorrhianus*, Italian translation by Edoardo D'Angelo (Turin: Edizioni dell'Orso, 2001), 113.

was elected pope with the name Benedict X (1058-1059), St. Peter Damian and the majority of the cardinals accused him of simony and declared anathema those who participated in that election. The group of reformers headed by Peter Damian and Hildebrand of Sovana (later Pope Gregory VII) elected another pope in the person of Nicholas II (1059-1061). Benedict X was tried and deposed at the Lateran in April 1060, based on the charge of perjury and simony, then divested of all ecclesiastical dignity and declared an antipope.[63] So he is considered today, but for a long time he was considered a legitimate pope and included in the catalogues of Roman Pontiffs, so that Niccolò Boccasini, elected to the papal throne in 1303, decided to call himself Benedict XI.[64]

Paschal II (1099-1118) allowed King Henry V in 1111 to extort from him the treaty of Ponte Mammolo, which granted to the king the investiture with ring and pastoral staff of imperial prelates before their episcopal consecration, thus adopting as his own the concession that Gregory VII had so decisively rejected in the conflict over investitures.[65] The opposition of the bishops, such as St. Bruno, Bishop of Segni and a monk from Montecassino,[66] was so vigorous that, in the Lateran Synod of 1112 the pope found himself forced to withdraw the privilege that he had conceded to the king, which his adversaries called a "*pravilegium*" [depraved privilege], and to adhere explicitly to the principles of his predecessors Gregory VII and Urban II.

Therefore, the popes accepted criticism and listened to the frank remonstrances made against them. Hergenröther recalls that "Paschal II humbly accepted in 1111 the reproaches against him; Eugene III—

---

[63] Hergenröther, 4:8.
[64] Benedict XI was beatified in 1738. *Cf.* the articles by O. Capitani, DBI, VI (1966), 366-370; Ingeborg Walter, in EP, II, 493-500.
[65] Hubert Jedin, *Breve storia dei Concili* (Brescia: Morcelliana, 2006), 61.
[66] See his letter from the year 1111 to Paschal II, in PL 163, 463: "*Audio Salvatorem meum mihi dicentum: 'qui amat Patrem aut Matrem plusquam me, non est mihi dignus' (Mt. X). Unde et Apostolus dicit: si quis non diligit Dominum. Debeo igitur diligere te, sed plus debeo diligere illum, qui et te feci et me.... Illi enim soli catholici, qui catholicae Ecclesiae fidei et doctrinae non contradicunt.*"—"I hear my Savior saying to me: 'He who loves father and mother more than me is not worthy of me' (Mt. 10). Hence the Apostle too says: 'Unless someone loves the Lord....' I must therefore love you, but I must love more the one who made both you and me.... The only Catholics are those who do not contradict the Faith and doctrine of the Catholic Church."

the admonitions of St. Bernard,[67] Hadrian IV—those of John of Salisbury (*Policraticus*, VI, 24), Innocent IV—the bold memorandum by Bishop Robert of Lincoln."[68] The dogmatic principle *Ubi Petrus ibi Ecclesia* did not rule out the possibility of critiques of the popes out of love for the Church of Christ of which they were not always worthy vicars. "The axiom, 'Where the pope is, there is the Church,'" Cardinal Journet writes, "is valid when the pope behaves like the pope and head of the Church; otherwise the Church is not in him, nor is he in the Church."[69]

The successor of Pope Paschal II, Callixtus II (1119-1124), after putting an end to the battle over investitures with the Concordat of Worms (1122), had this treaty confirmed by the Ecumenical Lateran Council I (1123), the ninth in the history of the Church and the first of the five held in the great building complex of the Lateran, which included the cathedral church of Rome and, for around a millennium, also housed the Apostolic See. This Council was important not only because it settled the centuries-old problem of investitures, but because it contributed to the reform of the Church with its renewed condemnation of simony and with its disciplinary decrees on ordinations and ecclesiastical offices.[70] This work was continued by the Lateran Councils II (1139), III (1179), and IV (1215) and by the First and Second Councils of Lyons (1245, 1274). The Second Council of Lyons affirmed the Catholic doctrine on the Primacy of Peter and the fullness of the Roman Pontiff's authority, which is one of the cardinal points of Catholic Tradition.[71] Taken together, the five medieval Councils withstood the heresies that were creeping through Christendom (above all the Cathari and the Waldensians), granted indulgences to crusaders, and took important measures on the doctrinal, disciplinary, and pastoral level.

Medieval civilization, according to Hergenröther, reached its apogee during the pontificate of Innocent III (1198-1216).[72] Lothario,

---

[67] St. Bernard, in *De Consideratione*, dictates to the newly elected Pope Eugene III the rules of the Pontificate, proposing to him a program for reforming the Curia inspired by the Gregorian tradition (PL 182, 727-808).
[68] Hergenröther 4:187.
[69] Charles Journet, *L'Église du Verbe Incarné*, 1:596.
[70] DH 710-712.
[71] DH 861.
[72] Hergenröther, 4:2.

a descendent of the Counts of Segni, a Pontiff who reestablished the authority of the Church, revived religious sentiment in Christendom, aided the crusaders to the East, vigorously opposed the new heresies, with the institution of the tribunal of the Inquisition as well. Despite his greatness, he was not without his faults, if it is true that St. Lidwina of Schiedam—the mystic who, as Hergenröther reports, "bore in her miserably wracked and almost deformed body the evils of the Church, but shortly before her death flourished again with unusual freshness"[73]—saw him in a vision condemned to Purgatory until the end of the world.

The apogee of the pontificate of Innocent III was the convocation of Lateran Council IV, which opened in November 1215 in the presence of around 1200 bishops, abbots, superiors of religious orders, and representatives of all the States of Christendom. Seventy canons about faith, customs, and discipline were issued, among them the principle that there is no salvation outside the Catholic Church.[74]

Benedict VIII (1294-1303), Benedetto Caetani, was the last great pope of the Middle Ages. The Bull *Unam Sanctam* dated November 18, 1302, in which "we declare, state, and define that it is absolutely necessary for the salvation of all human creatures that they submit to the Roman pontiff,"[75] is a manifesto of papal authority that has imperishable value. This act cost him the outrageous Affair of Anagni (1303) perpetrated by Philip the Fair, a deed that turned upside down the fundamental act of Christian civilization: that Christmas Eve in the year 800 in which, in St. Peter's Basilica, Charlemagne had knelt before Pope St. Leo III, acknowledging the latter's supreme authority. Hergenröther, while acknowledging the greatness of Pope Boniface, maintains that "the decisions that he made in the heat of the struggle were not always guided by the requisite prudence."[76] The consequences of the insult in Anagni however were devastating: the Great Western Schism which at the end of the 14th century tore Christendom apart, ensued from the Avignon exile of the popes, and this was in turn the final act of the war of Philip the Fair against the Roman Church.

---

[73] *Ibid.*, 2:364.
[74] DH 802. (*Una vero est fidelium universalis Ecclesia, extra quam nullus omnino salvatur.*)
[75] DH 875.
[76] Hergenröther, 4:323.

6. The Avignon crisis and the "Great Western Schism"

The Archbishop of Bordeaux, Bertrand de Got, ascended the papal throne with the name of Clement V (1305-1314), at the death of Boniface VIII. Since he had connections with Philip the Fair, Clement V gave in to pressures from him, condemning the Templars at the Council of Vienne, which was held between 1311 and 1312 in the Dauphine. The Council, the fifteenth in the Church's history, while not promulgating a theological judgment, suppressed by an act of papal authority the Order which had covered itself with glory on the battlefields of the Crusades and whose conspicuous assets the king of France coveted at that time. In August 1308, Clement V established the papal residence in the city of Avignon. It was supposed to be a temporary home but lasted 70 years. Regarding the sad period of Avignon (1308-1378), Cardinal Hergenröter wrote that: "not all popes, among the constant upheavals, could correctly understand the duties of their office and the needs of the times…Hence, the weakness of the Church in its center extended, so to speak, to all points of its circumference."[77]

The moments of weakness and defection concerned not only the exercise of government but also doctrine. John XXII (1316-1334) was elected pope in Lyon, after the See had remained vacant for almost two years. He upheld, as a private scholar, the heretical thesis according to which the righteous, after death, do not enjoy the beatific vision of God until the universal judgment.[78] "More than others," Cardinal Schuster later commented, "John XXII has serious responsibilities before the court of history…One can disregard the sometimes quibbling and rather childish disputes with the Franciscans about seraphic poverty, the possessions of the convents, the ownership and use of the produce, the question of whether or not Jesus Christ and the apostles had possessions in common; but when the pope, at first in writing, then from the pulpit, albeit as a private theologian, started to maintain that the souls of the dead cannot enjoy the vision of the divine Essence until the day of the last judgment, he offered the whole Church the humiliating picture of princes, clergy and universities that had to put the pope back on

---

[77] Hergenröther, 5:2.
[78] *Ibid.*, 4:38-39.

the right track of Catholic theological tradition, which put him in the dire need of retracting what he had said."[79]

Five other French popes followed, one of whom, Urban V (1362-1370), a Benedictine monk of Cluny, was then beatified. The Avignon crisis was the inspiration for Ludwig von Pastor's *History of the Popes*. As the German historian describes it "the papal power and the general interests of the Church…were severely shaken"[80] by the transfer of the papacy to Avignon and he added that in that period "the papacy…could not maintain its former dignity." The full exercise "of the highest spiritual authority" was rendered difficult and often impossible because "the freedom and independence of the popes was endangered."[81]

Under the Avignon popes, the prestige of the papacy weakened more and more, and if on January 13, 1377, the papal See was definitively returned to the Eternal City, it was mainly due to the insistent solicitations of two strong women of the Middle Ages, St. Catherine of Siena and St. Bridget of Sweden. St. Catherine, in her letters to Gregory XI (1370-1378), described to him, in trembling words, the bleak state of Rome and the decadence of the clergy's morals. Perhaps no one loved the papacy as vibrantly as she did, and precisely for this reason she spared no criticism in her exhortations to the Supreme Pontiffs.

St. Catherine of Siena addressed a high-ranking prelate, whose name we do not know, with these words:

> The shepherds are asleep in their own self-love, in cupidity and filth: they are so intoxicated with pride that they sleep and feel nothing, even when they see that the devil, infernal beast, is stealing the life of grace from them and their subjects…I see that, because they are silent, the world is rotten, the bride of Christ is pale, deprived of her color, because they have sucked the blood from her, thus the blood of Christ, which was given by grace and not by debt; they abandoned Him for pride, taking away the honor that should belong to God and giving it to themselves; they steal by simony, selling the

---

[79] Ildefonso Schuster, O.S.B., *Gesù Cristo nella storia: Lezioni di storia ecclesiastica* (Rome: Benedictina Editrice, 1996), 116-117.
[80] Pastor, 1:82.
[81] *Ibid.*, 1:75.

gifts and graces that were bestowed upon us by grace, at the price of the blood of the Son of God.[82]

A few months after his return to Rome, Gregory XI died on March 27, 1378. Fearing that the new pope could return to Avignon, the Roman people insistently demanded that a Roman pope be chosen, or at least an Italian one. The one elected was Bartolomeo Prignano, Archbishop of Bari, who took the name of Urban VI (1378-1389). However, a few months later, also because of the excessively imperious character of the new Pontiff, a group of cardinals, mostly French, denounced the conclave as invalid, because of the undue pressure put on it, and called for a new one to be held in Gaeta. Robert of Geneva was then elected, who took the name of Clement VII (1378-1434); he moved back to Avignon, declaring Urban VI deposed. The latter remained in Rome, with his own papal court, excommunicating the antipope. From 1378 on, Christianity found itself divided by the "Great Western Schism": one part of the Christian nations remained loyal to Urban VI; others recognized Clement VII. The countries proclaiming their "obedience" to the first were: Northern Italy, Germany, Central Europe, Scandinavia and England; while France, Spain and Scotland sided with the latter on the papal throne.

Urban VI, today recognized as the canonically legitimate pope, was succeeded by Boniface IX (1389-1404), Innocent VII (1404-1406) and Gregory XII (1406-1415). At the same time, Clement VII, who died in 1394, was succeeded by the Spaniard Pedro de Luna, who reigned for 22 years with the name of Benedict XIII (1394-1422).

"A division like the one that started in year 1378 had never been seen before in the Christian world,"[83] wrote Ludwig von Pastor; he noted that even though there had been antipopes previously in the Church's history, this time the schism had not been caused by the civil power, as in the days of the Hohenstaufens and of Ludwig the Bavarian, but rather by the cardinals themselves and the high-ranking clergy. Furthermore, the election of Urban VI had taken place in such unusual circumstances that it was not difficult to hide or

---

[82] Caterina da Siena, "Lettera a un gran prelato," in: *Lettere a Papi e a cardinali*, ed. Giuseppe Pensabene (Rome: Volpe, 1968), 137.

[83] Pastor, 1:145.

misrepresent the truth.[84] "A later generation which has many documents available and can survey the subsequent course of those events cannot judge how difficult or impossible it was for the men of that time to know which one of the candidates was the true and legitimate pope."[85]

Ubi Petrus, ibi Ecclesia: but where was Peter at the end of the 14th century? For over 40 years, European Catholics lived through a daily drama. Not only there were two colleges of cardinals, but often in the same diocese there were two bishops, two abbots, two parish priests. Every believer was in fact excommunicated by at least one pope.[86] Opposite St. Catherine of Siena and St. Bridget of Sweden were St. Vincent Ferrer and Blessed Peter of Luxembourg, adhering to the French obedience. The German historian also wrote: "There was a confusion without borders. Therefore, it was no surprise that the Christian religion became object of ridicule by Jews and Muslims."[87]

St. Catherine of Siena found herself experiencing two tragedies of the Church: first, the transfer of the papacy to Avignon, then, in the aftermath of the pope's return to Rome, which she had so much hoped for, the Great Western Schism, which saw Christianity split in two for 40 years, because it was impossible to tell which one was the legitimate pope. St. Catherine died, two years after the Schism exploded, without seeing the solution of it, but with the unshakeable trust that the Church would overcome this seemingly hopeless crisis.

St. Joan of Arc experienced an equally tragic personal situation, condemned to the stake as a heretic by ecclesiastical judges. Yet, despite the immense difficulties she encountered in her life, as a simple lay person facing theologians and doctors who accused her of witchcraft, she never gave up her mission, she let herself be guided by the Holy Spirit and today she is venerated as a saint by the Church. Benedict XVI described St. Catherine of Siena and St. Joan of Arc as "perhaps the most representative of those 'strong women' who, at the end of the Middle Ages, fearlessly bore the great light of the Gospel in the complex events of history. We could liken them to the holy

---

[84] *Ibid.*
[85] *Ibid.*, 146.
[86] St. Antoninus, *Chronic.*, tit. XXII, c. 11. "*non videtur saluti necessarium credere istum esse vel illum, sed alterum eorum.*" "It does not seem necessary for salvation to believe that this one or that one is [pope], but either of them."
[87] Pastor, 1:149.

women who stayed on Calvary, close to the Crucified Jesus and to Mary his mother. Mary, who remained while the apostles had fled and Peter himself had denied Him three times."[88]

In the dramatic times in which they lived, the two saints were guided by the light of faith much more than the theologians and ecclesiastics of the same era, and the pope applies to them the words of Jesus: the mysteries of God are revealed to those who have the heart of the little children, while they remain hidden to the learned and wise who do not have humility (Lk. 10:21). St. Catherine, according to Pastor, was for the papacy what the Maid of Orléans had been for the French monarchy.[89] In the kingdom of God, according to St. Thomas, all men and women are called to be saints and apostles. "In God's eyes even women fight, for many a woman has waged the spiritual warfare with the courage of a man. For some have rivaled men in the courage with which they have suffered martyrdom; and some indeed have shown themselves stronger than men."[90]

7. The Councils of the 15th Century

The chaotic situation in which the Church found itself at the beginning of the 15th century induced many cardinals of the two factions to seek a solution in a General Council that opened in Pisa on March 25, 1409.[91] The Council of Pisa, after being declared ecumenical and representative of the whole universal Church, deposed the two rival Pontiffs, Gregory XII and Benedict XIII, as "schismatic and heretical" and declared the Roman See vacant.[92] The participating cardinals, on June 26, then elected a third pope, in the person of the Archbishop of Milan, Pietro Filargo, who took the name of Alexander V (1409-1410), who was succeeded the following year by Baldassarre Cossa, with the name of John XXIII (1410-1415).

Alexander V had as little legitimacy as the Pisan council itself, as this was neither convened by any pope, nor presided or approved by one.[93] Yet, the situation did not appear clear for a few centuries:

---

[88] Benedict XVI, General Audience, 26 January 2011, at http://w2.vatican.va/content/benedict-xvi/en/audiences/2011/documents/hf_ben-xvi_aud_20110126.html
[89] Pastor, 1:151.
[90] St. Thomas Aquinas, *Summa theologiae* III, q. 72, art. 8, ad 3.
[91] Hergenröther, 5:140-147.
[92] Pastor, 1:198-199.
[93] Hergenröther, 5:147; Pastor, 1:199.

the portrait of Pietro Filargo appears in the series of popes in St. Paul's Basilica and the next pope who took the name Alexander, the Spaniard Rodrigo Borgia, called himself "the Sixth," legitimizing his predecessor. The *Historical Dictionary of the Papacy* includes an article on Alexander V as a pope, without questioning his legitimacy, while considering his successor John XXIII an antipope.[94] St. Robert Bellarmine, for his part, was convinced that both Alexander V and John XXIII were true Pontiffs.[95] This goes to show how often the legitimacy or illegitimacy of the popes was debated in the Church: problems not always immediately clear to the theologians and the faithful.

After the failure of the Pisan attempt, the Emperor of the Holy Roman Empire, Sigismund, took the initiative for a new Council that opened in the imperial city of Constance[96] on November 5, 1414, in the presence of the illegitimate Pope John XXIII and many prelates from all parts of Europe. The Council, which had as it primary objective the unity of the Church, was attended also by Cardinal Giovanni Dominici, as legate of the legitimate Pope, Gregory XII.

When John XXIII understood that the Council did not intend to confirm him as the pope, he fled from Constance on the night between March 20 and 21,1415, but was later captured, deposed as guilty of simony and a public sinner, and excluded, like the other two popes, from the future election. On April 6, 1415, the assembly then issued the decree known as *Haec Sancta*, in which it was solemnly affirmed that the Council, assisted by the Holy Spirit, represented the whole Church Militant and received its own power directly from God: therefore, every Christian, including the pope, was obliged to obey.[97] *Haec Sancta* was one of the most revolutionary documents in the history of the Church, because it denied the primacy of the Roman Pontiff over the Council. This text, at first recognized as authentic and legitimate, was subsequently rejected by the papal Magisterium.

---

[94] Cf. Hélène Millet, art. "Alessandro V," in *Dizionario Storico del Papato* [DSP], 30-31.

[95] St. Robert Bellarmine, *De Conciliis et Ecclesia*, Lib. I, cap. VIII, in: *De Controversiis christianae fidei, op. cit.*, vol. II, col. 12.

[96] On the Council of Constance, besides Hergenröther 5:157-184, see Léon Cristiani, "Constance," in DDC, IV (1949), cols. 390-424. G. Fornaseri (Giorgio Falco), *La Santa Romana Repubblica* (Naples: Ricciardi, 1942), 316-356.

[97] Text of *Haec Sancta* in Mansi, XXIX, cols. 21-22.

Gregory XII (the legitimate pope, who had been deposed by the Council Fathers of Constance,) sent a plenipotentiary to the assembly to declare his willingness to resign, provided that a Bull of his, in which he convened the Council, was first to be read publicly, as it indeed happened. The pope, forced to resign due to the unsustainable situation that had arisen, nevertheless salvaged the principle. The resignation was officially accepted on July 4, 1415, by the synodal assembly, which at the same time deposed the other antipope, Benedict XIII.[98] This one refused to resign but was then abandoned even by the countries of his obedience and deposed on July 26, 1417, as a perjurer, schismatic, and heretic. A new Pope, Martin V (1417-1431), Oddone Colonna, was then elected on November 11, 1417; shortly before leaving Constance, he confirmed the acts of the Council and, in compliance with the decree *Frequens*, called for the next Council to be held five years later in Pavia.

The Council of Pavia-Siena is not considered one of the Ecumenical Councils, but its contemporaries had no doubt about the ecumenical character of the assembly, and an influential historian of the contemporary Church, Cardinal Walter Brandmüller, maintains that it was, because it was unequivocally convened as such by the pope, who then ratified and promulgated its decrees.[99] However, the fruits of the Council, beyond its legitimacy, were almost nonexistent and after seven years, as established by the decree *Frequens,* on July 23, 1431, a new Council opened in Basel, under the successor of Martin V.

The conclave that followed the death of Martin V had imposed on its members a clause that entrusted the control of the Church's government and also a part of its revenues to the cardinals: this surrender of pontifical rights was ratified by the newly-elected Pope, Eugene IV (1431-1447), the Venetian Gabriele Condulmer, who ended up presiding at the Council convened by Martin V in Basel.

Toward the Council Fathers, Martin V struck an ambiguous and contradictory attitude. From the first sessions, they renewed the decrees of Constance that affirmed the superiority of the Council over the pope.[100] The Pontiff, with a Bull dated December 18, 1431,

---

[98] Pastor, 1:183.
[99] Walter Brandmüller, *Il Concilio di Pavia-Siena 1423-1424: Verso la crisi del conciliarismo* (Siena: Cantagalli, 2004).
[100] Hergenröther, 5:229 ff.

decreed the dissolution of the assembly but, given the threat of a new schism, he backed off and recognized the legitimacy of the Council, allowing it to continue.[101]

In Basel, Hergenröter recalls, those claiming the superiority of the Council over the pope were the eloquent Cardinal Cesarini, the young Enea Silvio Piccolomini (the future Pope Pius II), the theologian Nicholas of Cusa, and practically all the most famous doctors from the universities, with rare exceptions, such as the Spanish Dominican Giovanni Torquemada: "The science [of theology] seemed to have reduced forever the authority of the pope to a mere ministerial authority and the constitution of the Church to an authority that had features of both aristocracy and democracy."[102] Not until September 18, 1438, did Eugene V decide to transfer the Council to Ferrara, and then to Florence, but without ever denying the legitimacy of the Council of Basel. However, only a minority of the Council Fathers accepted the papal decree. The majority remained in Basel where on June 25, 1439, the assembly excommunicated and deposed Eugene IV and elected as pope Amadeus VIII of Savoy, with the name of Felix V.

The Council of Ferrara, then continued in the city of Florence, was the 17th Ecumenical Council of the Church. A large Greek-Orthodox delegation participated in it, led by the Emperor John VIII Palaeologus and the Patriarch of Constantinople Joseph II with his clergy. In Florence, Eugene IV solemnly sanctioned the reunification of the Eastern Church with Rome's and, on September 4, "*sacro approbante concilio*" ["with the Sacred Council approving"], condemned Basel's interpretation of the Council of Constance and proclaimed the doctrine of the pope's supreme authority, solemnly defining that "the holy Apostolic See and the Roman pontiff have the primacy over the whole world and that the same Roman pontiff is the successor of blessed Peter, the prince of the apostles and the true vicar of Christ, the head of the whole Church, the father and teacher of all Christians; and that to him, in the person of the blessed

---

[101] *Ibid.*, 5:234.
[102] *Ibid.*, 5:239.

Peter, was given by our Lord Jesus Christ the full power of feeding, ruling, and governing the whole Church."[103]

The "small" Western Schism (1378-1417) that followed the "Great" one was mainly caused by the vacillation of Eugene IV, who did not have the strength to condemn, from the beginning, the errors of the Council Fathers of Basel: his fear of provoking a schism by an attitude that was too firm was in reality the cause of the new fracture, which prolonged the crisis in the Church for another 20 years.

Sixty years of tragic confusion for the Church passed from the return of the papacy to Avignon until the Council of Florence. Cardinal Hergenröther recalls that, in that painful era, the examples of very worthy and even saintly bishops and priests were nonetheless never lacking: in Italy St. Andrew Corsini, Bishop of Fiesole; Blessed Giovanni Dominici, Archbishop of Ragusa; St. Lawrence Justinian, first Patriarch of Venice;[104] St. Antonino, Archbishop of Florence. Among the new religious orders were the Oblates of Tor de' Specchi, founded by St. Frances of Rome, and the Minim Friars of St. Francis of Paola, who was revered by popes and kings for his holiness.[105] Outstanding among the traditional mendicant orders were the Franciscans of St. Bernardine of Siena and St. John of Capestrano, and among the Dominicans, St. Vincent Ferrer.[106] The Holy Spirit never ceased to assist the Mystical Body of Christ, even in times of great perplexity in the visible Church.

8. From humanism to Protestantism

The era that followed the Western Schism was apparently more peaceful, but no less tragic than the previous one: in fact, it opened the doors to Martin Luther's Protestant Revolution.

---

[103] Denzinger-Hünermann, no. 1307. Contrary to what is stated in the Bull on Union with the Armenians *Exsultate Deo* (November 22, 1439), promulgated by the Council of Florence (Denz-H, nos. 1310-1328), Pius XII, in the Constitution *Sacramentum ordinis* dated November 30, 1947, (nos. 3857-3861) established that the imposition of hands and not the conferral of the chalice with wine and of the paten with bread is necessary for the validity of the sacrament of Holy Orders.

[104] Hergenröther, 5:343.

[105] *Ibid.*, 5:345-346.

[106] *Ibid.*, 5:348-349. I do not speak here about another famous Dominican, Girolamo Savonarola, because even though the cause for his beatification has been introduced, his attitude toward the Roman See is still controversial.

Humanism was born in Italy between the 14th and 15th centuries, a movement which, while proposing no open denial of Catholic truths, caused a real revolution in European mentality and customs: society was no longer centered on Jesus Christ but on a "new man" who replaced the love of God with the love of self as the predominant motive and favored earthly goods (pleasure, honor, wealth) over supernatural ones. It was the beginning of a process which, through logically consistent steps, would lead to the dissolution of Christianity.[107]

The head of pagan humanism can be considered, in Rome, Lorenzo Valla, who, while celebrating in his writings sensual pleasure as the highest good, was nevertheless secretary to popes and canon of the Lateran Basilica, where his tomb is located. In the brief pontificate of Innocent VII (Cosimo Migliorati, 1404-1406), Pastor already sees the new humanistic and worldly character of the Roman Curia asserting itself.[108] More and more humanists were at the service of the pope and among these, the German historian observes, "even some whose admission projects a sinister light on the conditions of those times."[109] Pastor cites the example of Poggio Bracciolini, who occupied the lucrative position of apostolic writer under eight popes, working in the Curia until 1453, for about half a century.

The 15th-century popes were at a dramatic crossroads, between the worldly spirit of humanism and the austere and combative spirit of the crusades. Nicholas V (Tommaso Parentucelli, 1447-1455) was among those who embraced humanism with the greatest enthusiasm, but under his pontificate distressing news arrived in the West about the fall of Constantinople and of the Byzantine Empire into the hands of the Turks.

Humanism meant cultural relativism and moral laxity. During the reign of Innocent VIII (Giovanni Battista Cybo, 1484-1492), the moral havoc, according to Pastor, reached the point where "after his death, because of the corruption, an Alexander VI could be elected."[110] "The salt of earth, for many reasons, had become taste-

---

[107] See a summary but magisterial analysis of this process in Plinio Corrêa de Oliveira, *Rivoluzione e Contro-Rivoluzione*, Italian translation edited by Giovanni Cantoni (Milan: Sugarco, 2009).
[108] Pastor, 1:173.
[109] *Ibid.*, 1:174.
[110] *Ibid.*, 3:144.

less, but where the purity of customs fades, even the Faith cannot remain intact," the German historian wrote,[111] adding that, in that period, "the immorality of the clergy was so great and widespread that voices were raised asking for the marriage for priests."[112] In the year of his death, during an Advent sermon, Innocent VIII had a dream that he considered divine revelation: a hand appeared to him with an unsheathed sword on which it was written: "*Gladius domini super terram cito velociter*"[113] "In a short time the sword of the Lord will strike the earth."

The Protestant Revolution was preceded, Hergenröther in turn writes, by "a time of profound degradation for the Apostolic See."[114] In the conclave of 1492 Cardinal Rodrigo Borgia was elected pope—validly "but by simoniacal intrigues"[115] with the name of Alexander VI (1492-1503). The German cardinal writes that throughout his life that man had thought of nothing but "to satisfy his passions, get wealthier and promote his own family" and "during his years as pope he continued that life style for a long time," "so that in the sight of the whole world his pontificate discredited the Holy See, which he profaned."[116] "His pontificate," Pastor concludes, "was a disgrace for the Church, on whose prestige he inflicted the deepest wounds."[117]

Alexander VI was succeeded by a soldier Pope, Julius II (1503-1513), Giuliano della Rovere, who with his cry "Out with the barbarians!" helped to foment Italian and foreign nationalism. On May 10, 1512, he convened Lateran Council V, to discuss the reform of the Church's life, which was characterized specifically by the appointment of unworthy prelates, the accumulation of benefices, failure by the bishops to comply with the residency requirement, and the infraction of clerical duties. The Council was continued by his successor, Leo X (1513-1521), the 38 year-old Giovanni de' Medici, a cardinal but not yet a priest at the time of his elevation to the papacy. Under his pontificate, in March 1517, the Lateran Council was concluded, few months before Martin Luther nailed his 95 theses on the door of

---

[111] *Ibid.*, 3:145.
[112] *Ibid.*
[113] *Ibid.*, 3:326.
[114] Hergenröther, 5:314.
[115] *Ibid.*
[116] *Ibid.*
[117] Pastor, 3:580.

the Wittenberg Cathedral. The Lateran Council V did not succeed in promoting the necessary reforms of the Church and can be considered a "failed Council," as it was clear from the words of the final decree announcing its closure. "Several times the cardinals and prelates of these commissions have reported us (Pope Leo X) that they had no more matters to discuss and examine and that, for several months, nobody had reported anything new to them."[118]

At the first news of the Protestant revolt, Leo X dismissed it as "a dispute among monks." Rarely in the history of the Church has there been such a great misunderstanding of the approaching storms. Pastor concludes the volume of his history dedicated to Leo X by affirming that his pontificate was "fatal to the Roman See."[119] "Being a man of frivolous and joyful character, he continued to indulge thoughtlessly in very mundane pleasures, even after the great storm had been unleashed that took a third of Europe away from the Roman See. In every respect a true son of the Renaissance, Leo X, surrounded by his artists, poets, musicians, comedians, buffoons and similar courtiers, abandoned himself with dreadful nonchalance to the whirlpool of worldly life, without caring whether or not his pleasures were fitting to a spiritual leader."[120]

The force of these words cannot be underestimated. Corruption had certainly been more serious under Alexander VI, a pope to whom no doctrinal errors can be attributed, but whose pontificate was "a disgrace for the Church, to whose prestige he caused the deepest wounds."[121] However, according to Pastor, the worldliness of Leo X was "more dangerous for the Church" because "it was much harder to fight."[122] The devastation caused by Luther and his followers in the Lord's vineyard was impressive. "The ancient Faith seemed extinct, the Apostolic See stripped of all authority, the episcopate condemned to die little by little."[123]

Yet, in this time of terrible trials, when no one spoke yet about Luther, ardently pious groups were born in the Church, called Companies of the Divine Love. The movement started in Genoa,

---

[118] COE, pp. 652-653.
[119] Pastor, 3:577.
[120] *Ibid.*, 3:575.
[121] *Ibid.*, 3:580.
[122] *Ibid.*, 3:576.
[123] Hergenröther, 6:222.

around St. Caterina Adorno de' Fieschi and had as its initiator a layman, Ettore Vernazza. In the course of a few years great reformers appeared, such as St. Gaetano of Thiene, founder of the Theatine Fathers, St. Philip Neri, founder of the Oratory, St. John of God, founder of the Brothers Hospitallers, St. Anthony Maria Zaccaria, founder of the Barnabites, St. Jerome Emiliani, founder of the Somascan Missionaries. The way of life led by the new religious orders was very similar: a strictly mortified life, the rejection of all worldliness, abandonment to Divine Providence, zeal for souls.

Then followed St. Angela Merici, founder of the Ursulines, St. Ignatius of Loyola, founder of the Jesuits, St. Vincent de Paul, founder of Congregation of the Mission or the "Vincentians," St. Francis de Sales and St. Jeanne de Chantal, founders of the Visitation, St. Teresa of Avila, reformer of the Carmelites. To write the history of the Church, one would need to know and tell the heroic deeds of these men and women, who reached holiness under the influence of the divine grace.[124] While Protestantism finally stopped making conquests, Dom Guéranger wrote, "God is pleased to show that the Roman Church has lost nothing because it preserved the gift of sanctity."[125]

9. The failed reform of Hadrian VI

The successor of Leo X, Hadrian VI (1522-1523), Adrian Florent, from Utrecht, was a "pious, wise and holy"[126] pope who was fiercely opposed by the Italian humanists for his moral rigor. Two things he held dear: the union of the Christian princes in order to fight the Turks and the reform of the Roman Curia,[127] but the brevity of his pontificate prevented him from completing his projects, in particular "the gigantic war against the abuses that deformed the Roman Curia and almost the whole Church."[128] Even if he had had a longer reign, the evil in the Church was too deeply rooted, Pastor notes, "for a single pontificate to be able to produce the great change that was

---

[124] Corrado Algermissen, *La Chiesa e le chiese*, Italian translation (Brescia: Morcelliana, 1942), 50-51.
[125] Dom Prosper Guéranger, "Le sens chrétien de l'histoire," in: *Jésus-Christ roi de l'histoire* (St.-Macaire: Association St.-Jérôme, 2005), 48.
[126] Pastor, 4/2:31.
[127] *Ibid.*, 4/2:61.
[128] *Ibid.*, 4/2:141.

necessary. All the evil that had been committed in several generations could be improved only with a long, uninterrupted process."[129]

Hadrian VI understood the severity of the evil and the responsibility of the men of the Church, as is clearly evident from an instruction which the Nuncio Francesco Chieregati read in his name at the Nuremberg Diet, on January 3, 1523. It was, as Ludwig von Pastor noted, a document of extraordinary importance not only as a record of the pope's reforming ideas, but also because it was an unprecedented text in the Church's history.[130]

After refuting the Lutheran heresy, in the last and most remarkable part of the instruction, Adrian deals with the defection of the supreme ecclesiastical authority in dealing with the innovators.

Here is the explicit instruction that he gave the Nuncio Chieregati:

> You may say, moreover, that God permits this persecution to be directed against His Church because of the sins of men, especially of the priests and the prelates of the Church; for it is certain that the hand of the Lord is not shortened that He cannot save, but our sins separate us from Him and hide His face from us so that He does not hear our prayers. The Scriptures complain that the sins of the people come from the sins of the priest, and, therefore (as Chrysostom says), our Saviour, when He was about to cure the sickness of the city of Jerusalem, went to the temple to chastise first of all the sins of the priests, like a good physician, who cures the disease by going to its root. We know that in this Holy See there have been many abominations these many years—abuses in spiritual matters, excessive decrees, and everything perverted; nor is there any wonder if the disease has descended from the head to the members, from the supreme pontiffs to other prelates of lower rank.
>
> All of us, prelates and ecclesiastics, have strayed from the right path, and for a long time there was no one who did good. Therefore we must all give glory to God and humble ourselves before Him: let everyone meditate on why he fell and strive to straighten up rather than be judged by God on the day of His wrath. For this reason you, in our name, will promise that we want to make every effort in order, first of all, to improve the Roman Curia, from which, perhaps, all these evil started; then, because the disease began from here, the recovery will also begin from here; we feel all the more obliged to accomplish this because everyone wants this reform. We never desired the papal dignity and would have more willingly closed

---

[129] *Ibid.*, 4/2:82.
[130] *Ibid.*, 4/2:86.

our eyes in the solitude of a private life: willingly we would have renounced the tiara, and only the fear of God, the legitimacy of the election and the danger of a Schism led us to assume the office of supreme pastor, which we do not intend to exercise out of ambition, or to enrich our relatives, but to restore to Holy Church, the bride of God, her former beauty, to help the oppressed, to raise up wise and virtuous men, in general to do all that is right for a good shepherd and for a true successor of St. Peter.

But let no one be surprised if we cannot eliminate all the abuses at once, since the disease has deep roots and has greatly spread. A step after another will be taken and at first the more serious and dangerous evils will be cured with appropriate medications so that a hasty reform of everything will not create even more confusion. Rightly, Aristotle said that every sudden change is dangerous to the republic....

The words of Hadrian VI recall those of St. Catherine of Siena and of many other reforming saints. Pastor explains:

Considered as a whole, the instruction shows that the pope did not derogate even to the smallest extent from a strictly ecclesiastical point of view. He distinguishes clearly and strictly the divine and the human element in the Church. The authority of the Church is founded exclusively on God: in matters of faith it is infallible. Its members however are subject to human corruption and all, the good as the bad, must not shy away from confessing their faults to God, from that confession that every priest, even the holiest, must make on the steps of the altar, before offering the sacrifice of the Mass. Hadrian, as a Pontiff, made that confession openly, solemnly and resolutely before the whole world, as an atonement for the sins of his predecessors and as a promise for a better future. Firmly convinced of the divine character of the Church, he, precisely for this reason, had no fear of speaking openly, but full of sorrow for the scandals and abuses in plain sight that disfigured its external appearance.[131]

Hadrian VI was succeeded by Giulio de' Medici, with the name of Clement VII (1523-1534). Under his weak pontificate, on May 6, 1527, the terrible sack of Rome took place, by the Lutheran *Landsknechte* [mercenary soldiers] of the Emperor Charles V. It is difficult to describe the extent of the devastation and the number of sacrileges committed.[132] "Hell is nothing compared to the view that Rome offers," can be read in a secret report dated May 10, 1527,

---

[131] *Ibid.*, 4/2:87-89.
[132] *Ibid.*, 4/2:253-275.

cited by Pastor.¹³³ The unlimited license to kill and rob lasted eight days. They raged with particular fury against ecclesiastical persons: nuns were raped, priests and monks killed or sold as slaves, churches, palaces and houses destroyed. Only after the terrible sack did the life of Rome change profoundly: the luxury and frivolity of the past disappeared and the general misery gave a severe and gloomy aspect to the sacred city.¹³⁴

We will have to wait for the pontificate of Paul IV (Giampaolo Carafa, 1555-1559) and, above all, St. Pius V (Michele Ghislieri, 1566-1572) to find a new, unbending and austere spirit on the throne of Peter. Clement VII deceived himself, thinking that he could confront the tragic religious crisis of his time with the arts of a Renaissance diplomat, but he, Pastor writes, lost sight of the spiritual mission of the papacy and with that its main element.¹³⁵ Even with regard to Henry VIII, "The hesitation of Clement VII did not correspond to the concept of the dignity of his office and brought harm to the cause of the Church."¹³⁶

Can some popes be, as historians write, "a disgrace for the Church" (Alexander VI), "fatal for the Roman See" (Leo X) or "harm the cause of the Church" (Clement VII)? Ludwig von Pastor does not hesitate to use those words, which do not affect the principle *ubi Petrus, ibi Ecclesia*. Love and respect for the institution do not mean an unconditional approval of the government actions of its supreme leaders. That would be to do an injustice to the truth of which they themselves are the supreme Vicars.

10. From the Council of Trent to the French Revolution

Between the second half of the 16th century and the first half of the 17th the Church experienced an era of doctrinal restoration and profound renewal of customs.

The Council of Trent, the 19th Ecumenical Council of the Church, was at the center of this great reforming effort. Sessions were held over the course of 18 years, from December 13, 1545, to

---

[133] *Ibid.*, 4/2:261.
[134] *Ibid.*, 4/2:324.
[135] *Ibid.*, 4/2:513.
[136] *Ibid.*, 4/2:513.

December 16, 1563, "to the praise and glory of God, to increase the faith and Christian religion, to eradicate heresies, for the peace and unity of the Church, for the reform of the clergy and of the Christian people, to confound the enemies of Christianity."[137] The Council made enormously important doctrinal decisions concerning Sacred Scripture and Tradition, original sin and justification; the Sacraments and the Sacrifice of the Mass. No less important were the disciplinary decrees that helped to develop that authentic Catholic reform which alone could oppose the Protestant pseudo-reform.

The Church is always demanding in raising candidates to the altars, and she is so especially for the popes; she must certify the heroism not only of their practical virtues but also of their practical virtues in the *munus* that is their own, the exercise of government. In the centuries that elapsed between the Protestant and the French Revolution there were many great popes, but the Church canonized only Pius V, and beatified only Innocent XI (Innocenzo Odescalchi, 1676-1689). To the first we owe the great victory of Lepanto against the Turks (1571) and to the second the liberation of Vienna and Hungary from Islam that was advancing in Europe (1683-1686). However, in those years, new errors became to germinate.

In 17th and 18th-century France a new heresy, Jansenism, began to spread. It was the first heresy that did not separate from the Church, but sought to change its doctrine and organization from within. The initiators of the movement, Jansen and St.-Cyran, died in peace with the Church, to which they were, apparently, faithful and submissive.

Along with Jansenism, an older error developed, Gallicanism, which in the Habsburg Empire took the name of Febronianism from the name of its promoter, Johann Nikolaus von Hontheim, known by his pseudonym of Justinus Febronius. The doctrine, condemned in 1764 by Clement XIII (1758-1769), was instead welcomed by the three most important prelates of the Empire, the elector archbishops of Mainz, Cologne and Trier and by the Emperor Joseph II himself (it was called Josephinism after him).

The responsibility for the errors that crept through the Church and the society fell on important ecclesiastical personalities, who spread them throughout Europe. As always, however, Providence

---

[137] Hergenröther, 6:233.

FROM TRENT TO THE FRENCH REVOLUTION

raised a handful of saints to promote the piety of the people and to oppose the errors of the time. We should mention the names, at least, of St. Louis-Marie Grignion de Montfort, the apostle of the Vendée, and of St. Alphonsus Liguori, apostle of Southern Italy and founder of the Redemptorists.

As in every period of struggle within the Church between the representatives of orthodoxy and those of heterodoxy, a "third party" formed which offered to mediate between the two opposing poles. In the 18th century, the exponent of the moderate "center" was Benedict XIV (1740-1758), Prospero Lambertini from Bologna. The papacy of Pope Lambertini, "however splendid," had for Hergenröter "its shadows in the great docility of the pontiff towards the governments of that time"[138] that adopted the principles of Gallicanism and jurisdictionalism. Docility toward the enemies of the Church was, over the course of history, the most recurrent error by those who are called to exercise the supreme authority of government. The first 37 popes in the history of the Church were all saints and almost all martyrs. In the second millennium, what characterized the few canonized pontiffs, none of whom had the glory of martyrdom, was the saintly intransigence with which they opposed the enemies of Faith and Christian civilization. The names of Gregory VII, Pius V and Pius X shine in the Church's firmament because of that militant spirit.

The Society of Jesus, founded by St. Ignatius, constituted an army at the service of the papacy, animated by a combative and ascetic spirit. In the 18th century, the enemies of the Church organized against it a true conspiracy in the literal sense, supported by the Bourbon courts. Clement XIV (1769-1774), the Franciscan Lorenzo Ganganelli, was elected pope on May 19, 1769, after a three-month conclave during which the King of France vetoed over 25 cardinals. Considered by Hergenröter "docile and liberal," he "took as his model Benedict XIV and exceeded him by far in his condescension towards the temporal governments."[139] Pastor passes a very severe judgment on his papacy. "Clement XIV," the German historian writes, "remains in the long list of popes as one of the weakest and most unfortunate."[140] Pope Ganganelli was accused of

---

[138] *Ibid.*, 7:195.
[139] *Ibid.*, 7:211.
[140] Pastor, 16/2:419.

having promised, during the conclave, the suppression of the Jesuits, which took place in 1773, with the Brief *Dominus ac Redemptor*, later annulled by Pius VII in 1814.[141] Pastor explains that it was not a "simoniac transaction," which would have invalidated the election, but it is certain that "the ambiguous attitude that Ganganelli had assumed as a cardinal on the matter of the Jesuits was kept by him even during the conclave."[142] The Brief *Dominus ac Redemptor* with which the pope dissolved the Society of Jesus is, according to Pastor, "the most obvious victory of royal Illuminism and absolutism over the Church and its leader."[143]

Did the Holy Spirit fail to assist the Church in that conclave or in others? The assistance of the Holy Spirit does not mean that the election of a pope enjoys "infallibility," just as it does not mean that the best candidate will be necessarily chosen in the conclave. If the election is valid, Cardinal Journet explains, even when it is the result of intrigue and bad choices, it is certain that the Holy Spirit, who assists the Church by turning evil too into good, allows such situations to happen for higher and mysterious purposes.[144]

The Brief *Dominus ac Redemptor* was a document issued by the supreme power of jurisdiction of the Roman Pontiff. It was therefore an authentic act of government, which the whole Church obeyed, but today it can be considered a wrong act with catastrophic consequences. The Society of Jesus, founded by St. Ignatius of Loyola, represented in fact a true and real defensive bastion of the papacy, to which its members took a vow of special obedience. Precisely because of its staunch defense of the Roman See, the Jesuits were hated by the main European courts, which had been corrupted by Gallicanism and Enlightenment philosophy. It was paradoxical that they were dissolved by the very same Roman Pontiff of whom they were the last line of defense. Predictably, the enemy then spread. Something similar had happened five centuries earlier, when Pope Clement V, instigated by the King of France, Philip the Fair, had suppressed the Templars, the first chivalric order of Christianity, similarly bound to the pope by a special vow of obedience. But while with regard to the Templars there were doctrinal and moral gray areas which could

---

[141] *Ibid.*, 16/2:412-421.
[142] *Ibid.*, 16/2:106.
[143] *Ibid.*, 16/2:223.
[144] Charles Journet, *L'Église du Verbe incarné*, 1:625.

lead an observer to presume that there was some form of infidelity to the original spirit, the same could not be said of the Jesuits, who were distinguished by their piety, doctrine and unwavering loyalty to the papacy. Their suppression opened the doors of the citadel to the enemy that was besieging it, at a time when, as Pastor writes, "Gallicanism and Jansenism, Febronianism and Josephinism, currents that also knew how to cover with beautiful words their hostility to the papacy, corroded the Church from within, as much as the spirit of the encyclopedists and of the 'philosophers' was threatening the Church from the outside."[145] Jansenism, Gallicanism, Regalism and the Enlightenment were different currents, but united by their anti-Roman spirit and by their hate for the Society of Jesus. Clement XIII, predecessor of Pope Ganganelli, on June 1, 1762, wrote to the King of France that the storm against the Jesuits would have toppled Throne and Altar. The prophecy came true with the French Revolution, which brought to its conclusion the process of de-Christianization initiated by humanism and by the Protestant pseudo-reform.

Faced with this new catastrophe, moments of weakness characterized the tormented pontificates of Pius VI (Gianangelo Braschi, 1775-1799) and Pius VII (Gregorio Chiaramonti, 1800-1823). Pius VI remained silent when, on July 12, 1790, the Revolutionary Assembly in France approved the schismatic Civil Constitution of the Clergy. Not until the following year, with the Briefs of March 10 and April 13, did he condemn the revolutionary constitution, at the time already signed by Louis XVI for lack of instructions from Rome.[146] On February 20, 1798, it was the same pope's turn to be expelled from the Vatican and from the Eternal City and exiled to Valence, France, where he died on August 20, 1799.

After seven months of *sede vacante*, Gregorio Chiaramonti, Bishop of Imola, was elected with the name of Pius VII. On July 15, 1801,[147] the new pope signed a Concordat with Napoleon, thinking that in that way he would conclude the era of the French Revolution, but Bonaparte soon showed that his real intention was to form a national Church subject to his power. On December 2, 1804,

---

[145] Pastor, 16/3:677.
[146] *Ibid.*, 16/3:509-614. On the Civil Constitution of the Clergy, *cf.* Jean Viguerie, *Christianisme et Révolution* (Paris: Nouvelles Éditions Latines, 1986), 73-113.
[147] *Concordato fra Pio VI e la Repubblica francese del 15 luglio 1801*, in Ench. Conc., nos. 1-19.

Napoleon crowned himself Emperor with his own hands and a few years later invaded Rome again, annexing the papal states to France. The pope was imprisoned and transferred to Grenoble and then to Savona (1809-1812).

On January 25, 1813, Pius VII, exhausted by the struggle with Napoleon, signed a pact known as "The Concordat of Fontainebleau"[148] in which, Hergenröther writes, he conceded "many things that seriously jeopardized the rights of the pope"[149]: he recognized, in fact, the alienation of his States and accepted the principle of submission to the French national authority. The Concordat placed the Church in the hands of the Emperor. Given the remonstrances of "zealous" cardinals, Pius VII, with great humility, recognized his error and, on March 24, signed a letter of recantation to Napoleon. There is nothing nobler, Leflon writes, than the confession of his weakness, expressed with these words: "It is our duty, and we make it a glory, in imitation of our predecessor Paschal II, to confess before God and the Church the error into which, as a man, we fell inadvertently."[150]

However, in Italy the pope's recantation was not immediately known, but only his signature of the Concordat. The venerable Pio Brunone Lanteri immediately composed a firm criticism of the pope's action, writing among other things: "Someone may tell me that the Holy Father can do everything, *'quodcumque solveris, quodcumque ligaveris etc.'* it is true, but he cannot do anything against the divine constitution of the Church; he is vicar of God, but he is not God, nor can he destroy the work of God."[151]

---

[148] *Concordato di Fontainebleau del 25 gennaio 1813*, in Ench. Con., no. 44-55.
[149] Hergenröther, 7:400.
[150] Declaration of Pius VII dated January 28, 1811, in: Jean Leflon, *La crisi rivoluzionaria (1789-1815)*, Storia della Chiesa, XVI, 1 (Turin: Editrice SAIE, 1982), 460. The text by Pius VII thus reads literally: "About that page, although signed by Us, we will say to Your Majesty the same thing that our Predecessor Paschal II had to say in the similar case of a letter signed by him containing a concession in favor of Henry V, of which his conscience had reason to repent, namely: 'since we recognize that that letter was badly written, we profess that it was badly written, and with the Lord's help we desire that it be corrected imminently, so that no damage to the Church and no harm to our soul may result from it'" (Ench. Conc., no. 45).
[151] Pio Brunone Lanteri, *Scritti e documenti d'Archivio*, II, *Polemici-Apologetici* (Rome-Fermo: Edizione Lanteri, 2002), 1019-1037 at 1024.

The venerable Lanteri, who was a staunch defender of the rights of the papacy, admitted the possibility of resisting the Pontiff in case of error, knowing that the power of the pope is supreme, but not unlimited and arbitrary. The pope, like any other believer, must respect the natural and divine law, of which he is the guardian by divine command. He cannot change the rule of faith, nor the divine constitution of the Church (for example the seven sacraments), just as the temporal sovereign cannot change the fundamental laws of the kingdom, because, as Bossuet recalls, when they are violated, "the foundations of the earth will be moved" (Ps. 81:5).[152]

No one could accuse Pio Brunone Lanteri of a lack of loyalty to the papacy: he was the founder of the Catholic League of Turin,[153] in which Count Joseph de Maistre, the great 19th-century apologist of the Roman Pontificate, distinguished himself.[154]

11. From Blessed Pius IX to St. Pius X

The 19th century was an era of great persecutions against the Church, promoted by Freemasonry and the secret societies, but it also witnessed a great renaissance of Catholicism after the devastation of the French Revolution. Most of the credit for this Catholic restoration belongs to Blessed Pius IX, Giovanni Maria Mastai Ferretti, whose long pontificate (1846-1878) illuminated the life of the Church by his solemn magisterial acts, such as the promulgation of the dogma of the Immaculate Conception (1854); the Encyclical *Quanta cura* and the *Syllabus* (1864) against the errors of his time; Vatican Council I, with its dogmatic definitions concerning the relationship between faith and reason and the primacy of the Roman Pontiff, who is declared infallible when he teaches "*ex cathedra,*" under certain conditions (1870). The pontificate of Pius IX should also be remembered for the extraordinary missionary expansion that brought the Gospel to every corner of the earth, during the same years in which the pope heroically defended the papal States, which

---

[152] Jacques-Benigne Bossuet, *Politique tirée des propres paroles de l'Écriture Sainte* (Geneva: Droz, 1967 [1709]), 28.

[153] *Cf.* Candido Bona, *Le "Amicizie": società segreta e rinascita religiosa* (Turin: Deput. subalpina di Storia Patria, 1962), and Roberto de Mattei, *La Biblioteca delle "Amicizie": Repertorio critico della cultura cattolica nell'epoca della Rivoluzione, 1770-1830* (Naples: Bibliopolis, 2005).

[154] Joseph de Maistre, *Du Pape* (Lyons: Rusaud, 1819), 2 vols.

were being attacked by the Kingdom of Sardinia and by the revolutionary secret societies.

Yet, Pius IX, who was a colossus of the Faith, in the first two years of his pontificate experienced hesitations and uncertainties.[155] Not until April 1848 did he, at the foot of the Cross, though aware of the suffering that lay ahead of him, make the decision not to give in to the revolution that was flattering him. From then on, his pontificate was an epoch of faith, in which he was joined by saints like Don Bosco, just one of the countless legion of souls who kept the Faith of the Church alive in the 19th century.

The great work of Ludwig von Pastor stops at the first years of the 19th century and Hergenröter's does not deal in depth with the pontificate of Leo XIII (1878-1903), from whom the German prelate received the purple hat. The Catholic historian who today, objectively, wants to consider that pontificate must recognize that Leo XIII had great merits: first of all, he restored dignity to the philosophy of St. Thomas Aquinas, with the Encyclical *Aeterni Patris* of 1879. But, in his exercise of the power of government, Leo XIII also committed errors, whose gravity emerged with the passage of time. The first was the *"ralliement"* with the Third French Republic, announced with the Encyclical *Au milieu des solicitudes* dated February 19, 1892, and confirmed on May 3 of the same year with a letter to the French cardinals. The document deserves to be criticized, but not because it seems to favor the republican form of government over the monarchy; we know well that the Church can agree with different forms of government, when they are founded on the natural and Christian order. The problem stems from the fact that the Pontiff hoped for an agreement with a regime, the Third French Republic, which was characterized by a deep-seated, anti-Christian secularism. The *ralliement* of Leo XIII was interpreted, beyond the intentions of the Pontiff, as the first "historical compromise" of the Church with the French Revolution, a hundred years after that catastrophic event. It was an act of "relaxation" that paved the way for that political modernism which had its first expressions in the

---

[155] *Cf.* Roberto de Mattei, *Pio IX* (Siena: Cantagalli, 2001), 28-56.

Sillon by Marc Sangnier in France and in the *Democrazia Cristiana* of Romolo Murri in Italy.[156]

When St. Pius X (Giuseppe Sarto 1903-1914) ascended the papal throne, the bark of Peter was already in the storm, and Pope Pius X, one of the greatest pontiffs in history, found, as he himself confessed, few faithful friends who supported him in his solitude. Pius X confided to Monsignore Alfonso Archi, Bishop of Como, "*De gentibus non est vir mecum*" ["There is not a man with me"] (Is. 63:3). The cross of his pontificate was the difficulty of facing the struggle with a few true and devoted collaborators, among them his Secretary of State Cardinal Rafael Merry del Val, with whom he led, *Cor unum et anima una* [with one heart and one soul], the anti-Modernist battle.[157] The abandonment of the struggle by the Italian episcopate had its origins in those years and runs throughout the 1900's . But already we are entering the 20th century, the century of totalitarian ideologies, but also of Vatican Council II (1962-1965), whose unwritten story I intended to narrate in the book which, in these pages, I wished to defend from rash accusations.

What I wanted to show is that the true Catholic does not get upset if the Faith is obscured for a few decades, even because of the defection of the highest ecclesiastical hierarchs. This does not mean that the Holy Ghost ceases to assist His Church. The Holy Ghost is for the Church what the soul is for the body, its vivifying principle, St. Augustine says and Leo XIII and Pius XII repeat with him.[158] The promise of the divine assistance of the Holy Ghost to the Church was often repeated by Lord to the apostles (Jn. 14:16-17; 14:25-26).[159] This divine assistance is not limited to the top of the hierarchy, but extends to every part of His Mystical Body, as Pius XII teaches in *Mystici Corporis*. Certainly, it is true that the main beneficiaries of

---

[156] For a picture of this period, see the groundbreaking work of Fr. Emmanuel Barbier, *Histoire du catholicisme libéral et du catholicisme social en France du Concile du Vatican à l'avènement de S.S. Benoît XV*, 5 vols. (Paris: Cadoret, 1923-1924).

[157] *Cf.* P. Girolamo Dal Gal, *Il servo di Dio card. Raffaele Merry del Val, Segretario di Stato di S. Pio X* (Rome: Paoline, 1956), 69-76.

[158] "*Quod autem est anima corpori hominis, hoc est Spiritus Sanctus Corpori Christi, quod est Ecclesia*," "What the soul is to the human body, the Holy Ghost is to the Body of Christ, which is the Church" (St. Augustine, *Sermo* 267, 4 in PL 38, 1231); Leo XIII, Encyclical *Divinum illud munus*, in: *ASS* 29 (1896/1897): 650; Pius XII, Encyclical *Mystici Corporis Christi*, in: *AAS* 35 (1943): 220.

[159] *Cf.* Michael Schmaus, *La Chiesa* (Casale Monferrato: Marietti, 1963), 312 ff.

this gift are the ministers of the teaching Church, and they are so especially at particular moments, such as Councils and conclaves, but this does not mean that those authorities automatically correspond to the grace. The grace of the Holy Ghost is not a magical virtue that gives power to those who receive it regardless of their collaboration. Docility, but also opposition to the action of the Holy Ghost characterizes the history of the Church since its inception. "It is in our power to snuff out or to kindle the flame of the Spirit; therefore another passage warns us: beware of extinguishing the Spirit (1 Thess. 5:19)."[160] St. Paul warned: *Spiritum nolite estinguere*: this warning echoes over the centuries.

12. The rock of Peter overcomes every storm

Both Cardinal Hergenröther and Baron von Pastor firmly believed, as we do, in the dogma of the universal primacy of the Roman Pontiff, including the privilege of infallibility; they believed, as we do, that when a Council, legitimately convened under the guidance of the pope, makes definitions in matters of faith and morality, its decisions must be religiously accepted, in the spirit of obedience; but Cardinal Hergenröther and Baron von Pastor knew that the pope is not infallible when he exercises his power of government or when he proposes a doctrine without defining it, and that infallibility presupposes special assistance by the Holy Ghost in carefully delimited acts; not all Councils are infallible and not in all of their acts and documents.

Hergenröther and Pastor knew, above all, that the Church is indefectible despite its children's faults and according to the promises of its Founder (Mt. 16:18; 28:20), that it will preserve the Faith until the end of time and will not lose any of its visible marks and properties that make it one, holy, Catholic and apostolic. The assistance of the Holy Ghost is guaranteed to the Church until the end of the world (Jn. 14:16) and the more serious the evils, the greater the reaction aroused by the divine Providence. In fact, Cardinal Hergenröther wrote, "the divine order takes revenge on its enemies. And the future will show this, as the past already demonstrated."[161]

---

[160] St. Jerome, *In Epist. II ad Tim.*, 1 (PG 62, 603).
[161] Hergenröther, 7:874.

Benedict XVI, in the aforementioned speech of December 22, 2005, using a metaphor of St. Basil, compared the post-conciliar era to a naval battle, at night, in a stormy sea, describing "the raucous shouting of those who through disagreement rise up against one another, the incomprehensible chatter, the confused din of uninterrupted clamouring."[162] This is the tragic era in which we live: an era that we must face with a sense of faith and a militant spirit.

Throughout its history, the Church has experienced external persecutions and internal crises and has always dealt with them with a militant spirit, because, the Book of Job says, the life of man upon earth is a warfare (Job 7:1), and so it is for the earthly existence of the Church. The Catholic historian, Dom Guéranger recalls, never forgets that the Bride of the Savior must carry on and justify, in this world, her glorious name of Church *militant*.[163]

There is however a fundamental difference between the persecutors of yesterday and those of today. Yesterday's persecutors wanted to eradicate Christianity without knowing the wonderful results that it would produce in history. Today's persecutors have before their eyes the historical fruits of Christianity: those fruits that are in front of our eyes, because everything tells us about the beauty, the greatness and the glory of Christian civilization, which is the greatness, the beauty, and the glory of the name of Christ, before whom Heaven and earth bow (Phil. 2:11-12). Today's persecutors also enjoy the support of "fifth columns" within the Church, which open the doors to the enemy, as happened in Rome when it was besieged by Alaric and in Constantinople when it was attacked by the Turks. But also the persecuted of today are different from those of yesterday, because those of yesterday carried in their hearts a promise that had not yet been fulfilled and bent their helpless heads before the executioners; the persecuted of today have the duty to defend, with all their intellectual and civil might, the Church and Christian civilization and to raise, with the standard of the Cross, the banner of Catholic Tradition.

The Church is still standing in the storms: heresies, scandals, revolutions, Dom Guéranger writes, have not shaken it or stopped its march in history: "Let us see therefore mankind in its relations

---

[162] St. Basil, *De Spiritu Sancto*, 30, 77 (PG 32, 213).
[163] Dom Prosper Guéranger, *Jésus-Christ roi de l'histoire*, 88.

with Jesus Christ, its guide; let us never ignore them, neither when we judge, nor when we relate the history; and when our eyes are fixed on the map of the world, let us remember first of all that we have before our eyes the empire of the Man-God and of His Church."[164]

"The rock of Peter," Ludwig von Pastor writes at the conclusion of his *History of the Popes*, "overcomes the storms of every century. The greatest and most inconceivable fact in the history of Christ's Church is that the times of its most profound humiliation are, at the same time, those of its greatest energy and invincible force, that death and the grave are for it not a sign of the end, but symbols of the resurrection, that the catacombs of early Church and anti-Christian persecutions of the contemporary one can therefore prove to be only a sign of glory...Christ, indeed, still walks with Peter on the rough waves and therefore these words still apply to the successors of the latter: '*tu es Petrus et super hanc petram aedificabo Ecclesiam meam, et portae inferi non praevalebunt adversum eam.*' ['Thou art Peter and upon this Rock I will build My Church, and the gates of hell shall not prevail against it.']"[165]

---

[164] *Ibid.*, 37.
[165] Pastor, 16/3:677-678.

II

The Church's *Regula Fidei* in Times of Crises of Faith

1. Benedict XVI and the hermeneutic of continuity

On October 12, 1962, a Council started that was destined to change profoundly, if not the essence of the Church, then certainly the face that she presented to the world and to her own sons and faithful. It was the 21st Ecumenical Council, but to many people it appeared to be the only and definitive one: a sort of watershed that divided the history of the Church and of humanity in two: before and after Vatican II.

Someone spoke about the end of the Constantinian era, to indicate the conclusion of a historical period that had started in the 4th century, when the Church had obtained her freedom from the Emperor Constantine and had commenced the Christianization of the ancient world. Now the Church was being asked to be open and docile and to offer no resistance to modern society, which was undergoing a process of de-Christianization—the reverse of the one that began under Constantine.

The history of the post-Conciliar period, even more than the period of the Council itself, remains to be written. But what is certain is that 20 years after the conclusion of those historic sessions, which ended on December 8, 1965, a major ecclesiastical figure who had been active at the Council, Cardinal Joseph Ratzinger, expressed his view in astonishing terms. In his book-length interview with Vittorio Messori entitled *The Ratzinger Report*, which appeared in 1985, Cardinal Ratzinger, who had become Prefect of the Congregation for the Doctrine of the Faith, used these words to describe the Church's situation:

> Developments since the Council seem to be in striking contrast to the expectations of all, beginning with those of John XXIII and Paul VI. Christians are once again a minority, more than they have ever been since the end of antiquity…What the popes and the Coun-

cil Fathers were expecting was a new Catholic unity, and instead one has encountered a dissension which—to use the words of Paul VI—seems to have passed over from self-criticism to self-destruction. There had been the expectation of a new enthusiasm, and instead too often it has ended in boredom and discouragement. There had been the expectation of a step forward, and instead one found oneself facing a progressive process of decadence that to a large measure has been unfolding under the sign of a summons to a presumed "spirit of the Council" and by so doing has actually and increasingly discredited it…The Church of the post-conciliar period is a huge construction site. But…it [is] a construction site where the blueprint has been lost and everyone continues to build according to his taste.[1]

Another 20 years later, the same Cardinal Ratzinger ascended to the papal throne with the name Benedict XVI. The *Via Crucis* [Way of the Cross] that he preached on the vigil of his elevation to the pontificate made a profound impression; in it, speaking to the whole world, he said: "How much filth there is in the Church, and even among those who, in the priesthood, ought to belong entirely to Him."[2] And the speech that he gave to the Roman Curia on December 22, 2005, during the first year of his pontificate, appeared to be a decisive one.[3] In it the pope clearly pointed out the path of a "reinterpretation" of Vatican II, which was presented by him in the form of the "hermeneutic of continuity." There has been much discussion about the meaning of these words. Yet the address of Benedict XVI posed but did not settle a problem: or rather, it demonstrated the existence of that problem while showing the path to follow in order to solve it, although he was aware of all the controversies that his statements would provoke.

Beyond the interminable discussions, the reality is that 50 years after Vatican Council II the Catholic Church is suffering one of the most terrible crises in her history. It is not just a matter of the growing persecution to which Christians are being subjected in every corner of the world. The distinctive marks of the Church, which show her

---

[1] Cardinal Joseph Ratzinger with Vittorio Messori, *The Ratzinger Report: An exclusive interview on the state of the Church*, translated by Salvator Attanasio and Graham Harrison (San Francisco: Ignatius Press, 1985), 29-30.
[2] *Idem. Via Crucis*, 25 March 2005, Meditation on the 9th Station, in: http://www.vatican.va/news_services/liturgy/2005/via_crucis/en/station_09.html
[3] Benedict XVI, Christmas Greetings to the Roman Curia (22 December 2005), http://w2.vatican.va/content/benedict-xvi/en/speeches/2005/december/documents/hf_ben_xvi_spe_20051222_roman-curia.html

to the world as one, holy, Catholic, and apostolic,[4] as we profess in the Creed, seem to be obscured to the point of making her unrecognizable to her own children.

Before being visible signs by which to recognize her, these characteristics of the Church are properties intrinsic to her. The Church has been, since her foundation, *one and undivided* in her worship, in her doctrine, and in her government; *holy and immaculate*, never sinful, although she contains sinners within her; *Catholic*, that is, universal, destined to spread throughout the world the unique salvific baptism of Christ; *apostolic*, because she is founded upon the uninterrupted succession of her pastors, from the apostles down to our days.

And yet, today the Church appears to the world to be no longer one, but fragmented in her doctrine, internally divided into trends and factions that fight among themselves; her face no longer seems pure and spotless, but covered with the grime that Benedict XVI described as "filth." She seems to have renounced her catholicity, in the name of an ecumenism that forgets her message of universal salvation; the one mark that still evidently survives is her apostolicity, which unites over time the popes and all the bishops in union with them, from St. Peter to Benedict XVI [as of 2011 when this book was written], but the threat of divisions and conflicts, as it happened in the Great Western Schism, weighs upon the bark of Peter, which nevertheless, according to the promise of its Founder, will never be submerged by the waves.

The Church, nevertheless, is not made up of theologians alone, but of all who profess the same Faith under their legitimate pastors. In eras of crisis of the Faith, every simple baptized person, guided by natural reason and enlightened by the *sensus fidei*, can obtain from the papal Magisterium and from Catholic Tradition sure criteria so as not to be swept away by the tempest, while remaining faithful to

---

[4] In the Niceno-Constantinopolitan Creed we profess our Faith "in one, holy, Catholic, and apostolic Church" (Denz-H 150). Cf. also the Bull *Unam Sanctam* by Boniface VIII (DH 870-875), the 1896 Encyclical *Satis Cognitum* by Leo XIII (DH 3303 ff.), and the 1943 Encyclical by Pius XII, *Mystici corporis Christi, quod est Ecclesia* (DH 3800-3822; *AAS* 35 [1943]: 193 ff.). The new *Catechism of the Catholic Church* reaffirms these marks as "essential features" of the Church and of her mission. It says: "The Church does not possess them of herself; it is Christ who, through the Holy Spirit, makes His Church one, holy, Catholic, and apostolic" (CCC 811-812).

the Church, about which it has been said, "*Tunditur, non mergitur*"[5]: she is buffeted, but she is not sunk, and there is no salvation outside of her.

2. The method of "the sources of theology"

A sure way to be guided in the Faith is offered to us by the method proposed by the Dominican theologian Melchior Cano[6] in his famous work *De locis theologicis*[7] (1562), which helped to rebuild the Church's theology after the devastations caused by Protestantism.

The *loci theologici* are the complete system of the sources of authority from which to begin, and which are to be followed when reasoning about matters of faith. According to Fr. Melchior Cano, there are ten "proper sources of theology," or the "domiciles of all theological arguments, from which theologians can take all the arguments needed both to prove and to refute." He enumerates them as follows:

> The first source is the authority of sacred Scripture, which contains the canonical books.
>
> The second is the authority of the traditions of Christ and of the apostles, which, even if they were not written, have come down to us orally, in such manner that in all truth they can be called *viva voce* oracles.
>
> The third is the authority of the Catholic Church.

---

[5] St. Peter Chrysologus, *Sermo* 21 (PL 52, 258 A).
[6] Melchior Cano, Dominican preacher and theologian (Tarancón 1509 – Toledo 1560). Professor in Alcalá (1541) and Salamanca (1546-1542); played an important part (1551-1552) at the Council of Trent in the discussions about Penance and the Eucharist. He was Provincial (1559) of Spain for his Order. About him see the article by P. Mandonnet in DTC, II, 2, cols. 1537-1540. The better contemporary theologians continue to cite his doctrine of the "*loci theologici.*"
[7] Melchor [thus in Latin and German] Cano, *De locis theologicis*, ed. Juan Belda Plans (Madrid: Biblioteca de Autores Cristianos, 2006). About this work see: Albert Lang, *Die Loci theologici des Melchor Cano und die Methode des dogmatischen Beweises: Ein Beitrag zur theologischen Methodologie und ihrer Geschichte* (Munich: Joseph Kösel und Friedrich Pustet, 1925); Cándido Pozo Sánchez, S.J., *Fuentes para la historia del método teológico en la escuela de Salamanca* (Granada, Facultad de Teología, 1962): A. Gardeil, "Lieux théologiques," in: DTC, IX, 1, cols. 712-747; Federico dell'Addolorata, "Luoghi teologici," in: EC, VII, cols. 1695-1697.

The fourth is the authority of the Councils, especially the General Councils, in which the authority of the Catholic Church resides.

The fifth is the authority of the Roman Church, which by divine privilege is and calls herself apostolic.

The Sixth is the authority of the Church Fathers.

The seventh is the authority of the scholastic theologians, to whom we can add the canonists (experts in Church law), inasmuch as the teaching of this law is considered another part of scholastic theology.

The eighth is natural reason, well known in all the sciences that are studied by this natural light.

The ninth is the authority of the philosophers who follow nature as their guide. Among these no doubt are the jurists (jurisconsults of the civil authority), who also profess the true philosophy (as the jurisconsult says).

The tenth and last is the authority of human history, both as written by reliable authors and as transmitted from generation to generation, not superstitiously or as old wives' tales, but seriously and coherently.[8]

None of these theological sources is absolute. If it is a question of defining a dogma or of establishing a theological truth with sufficient certitude, it is necessary for there to be a convergence among them and not an antithesis.

In order to be considered *de fide* [to be held by faith], a teaching must be first of all contained in sacred Scripture[9] and/or in Tradition,[10] the two "sources" that form the essential deposit of Revelation; moreover this teaching must be believed by the whole Church, which is the divinely instituted organ of Tradition, and, within the Church, must be confirmed and taught by the Councils and, above all, by the Roman Apostolic See.

The doctrine of faith, in order to be considered such, must also be supported by the testimonies of the Church Fathers[11] and of

---

[8] Melchior Cano, *op. cit.*, 9-10.
[9] *Ibid.*, 14-72.
[10] *Ibid.*, 175-217.
[11] *Ibid.*, 415-454.

the Scholastic theologians[12] and must not be contradicted by the "improper" [or "borrowed"] but real theological sources: natural reason,[13] which has its greatest expression in philosophy and in law,[14] and history,[15] which furnishes both certain and probable arguments to speculative theologians.

In this articulated framework, three points deserve to be emphasized and developed:

> 1) The role of Tradition which has, as we will see, primacy over all the theological sources, including sacred Scripture.
>
> 2) The concept of the Church as a totality, which includes the supreme teaching authority, which is expressed in the teaching of the pope and of the Council, but does not completely coincide with it.
>
> 3) The absence, among the theological sources, of the "Magisterium," which is absorbed by "sources" 4 and 5 (Councils and the pope): this does not mean that it does not exist or does not have its importance, but that it must be understood in its proper sense as a "power" or a "function" of the Church's supreme authority. The statement that the Church's Magisterium constitutes a *"regula fidei"* [rule of faith] and hence a *"locus theologicus"* [source of theology], is not wrong in itself, if it is understood as a power exercised by the teaching Church, in continuity with Tradition, of which the Church herself is the guardian. But those who repeat the argument that the Magisterium is the supreme *"regula fidei"* because it "interprets" Tradition, avoid confronting the problem posed by the existence of possible contradictions, real or apparent, between Tradition and the "current" ecclesiastical preaching, or "living" Magisterium. Obviously we are talking about exceptional cases in Church history, but what we want to examine more closely is precisely this, the "exceptional case": this occurs when we find ourselves facing a possible incompatibility, and therefore a difficult choice between Magisterium and Tradition. And here the theological system of Melchior Cano comes to our aid, helping us to confront the question in a rigorous manner.

---

[12] *Ibid.*, 455-492.
[13] *Ibid.*, 493-526.
[14] *Ibid.*, 527-552.
[15] *Ibid.*, 553-666.

3. The primacy of Sacred Tradition

Against the Protestants, who pitted Scripture against Tradition, thus falling into radical subjectivism, Cano, like all the theologians who followed him, stresses the logical and chronological priority of Tradition over Scripture. The canonical books—he recalls—in all their parts were written with the assistance of the Holy Spirit and therefore come directly from God. Nevertheless the deposit of Revelation is not entirely contained in Scripture because "the apostles did not transmit the whole doctrine of the Faith in writing, but a part of it through the spoken word."[16]

The theologian from Salamanca formulates four fundamental points which we reprint verbatim: a) the Church is older than Scripture and therefore the Faith and the Christian Religion exist without Scripture because the Church began to transmit the Word of God before it was gathered in the Sacred Books; b) not everything that belongs to Christian doctrine, including the things contained in Sacred Scripture, was formulated clearly; c) many things that belong to doctrine and to the Christian Faith are not contained in Sacred Scripture at all, either clearly or obscurely; d) the apostles, for reasons of the greatest importance, made some things known in writing and others *viva voce* instead.[17]

We will not dwell on these points because, after the Council of Trent, they are the infallible doctrine of the Church. We merely add that the primacy of Tradition over Scripture is due also to the fact that the Church was the one that exercised her discernment about the writings that circulated after Pentecost, distinguishing between the divinely inspired Gospels and the apocryphal ones, when in the mid-4th century she established to so-called Canon of Sacred Books, that is, the selection of those which, together with Tradition, would constitute the sources of our Faith.

Sacred Tradition can therefore legitimately be considered as a whole of which Sacred Scripture too is a part.

---

[16] *Ibid.*, 194.
[17] *Ibid.*, 184-186. Some dogmas are based on Tradition alone, for example the doctrine that Jesus instituted all seven Sacraments or that the pope is the Bishop of Rome, or the form of certain sacraments.

4. The Church and her spirit of truth

Three centuries before it was defined by Vatican Council I, Melchior Cano considered the authority of the pope a theological source.[18] He deems it infallible, not when the pope speaks as a private person or teacher, but when he addresses the universal Church and defines a doctrine of faith with the intention of obliging the faithful to believe it. Nevertheless, although he is a vigorous proponent of the universal Primacy of the Roman Pontiff, Cano distinguishes the authority of the pope and of the Councils at which he presides from the authority of the universal Church, considered as a "whole" of which the pope and the Councils are a part.[19]

Anticipating the teaching of *Mystici Corporis* by Pius XII, the Dominican theologian considers the Church a social body made up of all the baptized, the just and the sinners, united by the profession of the same Faith, under the legitimate ecclesiastical authorities. The word "Church" therefore designates both the pastors and the faithful people subject to them.[20] To this social body, considered in its entirety and comprising both the teaching Church and the learning Church, Melchior Cano attributes the characteristics of indefectibility and infallibility, as distinct from the infallibility that is reserved to the Roman Pontiff under certain specified conditions.[21] The Spirit of Truth is the soul of this body (Eph. 4:4), and if the Church is governed by the Spirit of Truth she cannot fall into error.[22] If that could happen, then the house of Christ would not in fact be "the pillar and ground [foundation] of the truth" (1 Tim. 3:15). The Church in her entirety is, for Cano, the first theological source that transmits and witnesses to Tradition.

---

[18] *Ibid.*, 359-414.
[19] *Ibid.*, 221-287.
[20] *Ibid.*, 250.
[21] *Ibid.*, 242 ff. *Cf.* also Juan Belda Plans, "La infalibilidad ex cathedra del Romano Pontífice según Melchor Cano: Estudio de las condiciones de la infalibilidad en cuanto al modo," in: *Scripta Theologica* 10 (1978): 519-575.
[22] Melchior Cano, *op. cit.*, 245.

5. The absence of the Magisterium from the theological sources

Among the theological sources listed by Melchior Cano we do not find the "Magisterium," a term that started to become widespread in theological language only in the 19th century.[23] The Magisterium, in fact, is not an autonomous theological subject in itself, but rather a power or, if you prefer, a "function" or office of the Church. Confronted with liberalism, many theologians wanted to strengthen the role of this power, proposing it as the "proximate rule" of the faith, as though it could sum up in itself the Church, the Councils, and the pope. It is significant, however, that the term "Magisterium" is found neither in the *Dictionnaire Apologétique de la Foi Catholique* by Fr. Adhemar d'Alés (1911-1922), nor in the famous *Dictionnaire de Théologie Catholique* (1909-1950), and not even in the equally well-known *Enciclopedia Cattolica* (1949-1954) promoted by Pius XII.

Given the attacks of Modernism, too, and then of the *Nouvelle Théologie*, it seemed urgent in the 20th century to stress vigorously the role of the Church's Magisterium.[24] It was from this perspective that Pius XII affirmed in the Encyclical *Humani Generis* that the authentic interpretation of the deposit of Revelation is not up to "individual believers, nor to the theologians themselves, but solely to the Magisterium of the Church."[25] In 1942, when two publications by the Dominican Fathers Louis Charlier and Marie-Dominique Chenu, exponents of the New Theology, were placed on the Index, then-Monsignor Pietro Parente deplored these two books for "their devaluation of the positive proofs from sacred Scripture and Tradition for theological theses, as well as their strange identification of Tradition (a source of revelation) with the living Magisterium of the

---

[23] It seems that the term appears for the first time in the Brief *Dum acerbissimas* by Gregory XVI dated September 26, 1835 (DH 2379). *Cf.* Dominique Le Tourneau, "La détermination du magistère ecclésiastique au long du deuxième millénaire," in: *Revue du droit canonique* 50/2 (2000): 263-281; Yves Congar, "Pour une histoire sémantique du terme 'magisterium,'" in: *Revue des Sciences Philosophiques et Théologiques* 60 (1976): 85-98.

[24] See for example Fr. Jean-Vincent Bainvel, S.J., *De magisterio vivo et traditione* (Paris: Beauchesne, 1905).

[25] Pius XII, Encyclical *Humani Generis* (September 9, 1950), in *AAS* 42 (1950): 569-578.

Church (the guardian and interpreter of the divine Word)."²⁶ During the pontificate of Pius XII, the tendency to identify the Magisterium improperly with Tradition was manifested in a series of articles by a Jesuit at the Gregorian University, Fr. Giuseppe Filograssi, which had remarkable repercussions in the theological discussion of that period.²⁷

Apart from the good intentions of the conservative theologians, the risk, which was foreseen by the future Cardinal Parente, was to identify the Magisterium with the Church, of which it is a power, placing it on the same level as Tradition, if not actually giving it priority over past teaching. The confusion was augmented by the Constitution *Dei Verbum* of Vatican Council II, which seemed to unify the two sources of revelation—Scripture and Tradition—with the Magisterium. In the summary formula Scripture-Tradition-Magisterium, Tradition, as Monsignor Gherardini observed, lost its force between the two pincers of Scripture and the Magisterium.²⁸ "The living Magisterium of the Church" became the sole organ of Tradition,²⁹ but this Magisterium, detached from the other theological sources and replacing them, became not the "proximate" but the sole rule of faith, the sole *locus theologicus*, the sole source of knowledge about revealed truth.

The doctrine of the theological sources taught by Melchior Cano and by many theologians who follow his method does not consider the Magisterium, because it is not a theological *locus*, "source," or "subject," but rather a function performed by the pope, by the Councils, and by the teaching Church within the power of jurisdiction.

---

²⁶ Pietro Parente, "Nuove tendenze teologiche," in: *L'Osservatore Romano*, February 9-10, 1942.

²⁷ Giuseppe Filograssi, "Tradizione divino-apostolica e Magistero della Chiesa," in: *Gregorianum* 33 (1951): 135-167; *idem*, "Traditio divino-apostolica et assumptio B. V. Mariae," in: *ibid.* 30 (1949): 443-489; "Theologia catholica et assumptio B.V.M.," in: *ibid.* 31 (1950): 323-350; see also Paul Nau, O.S.B., "Le magistère pontifical ordinaire lieu théologique," in: *Revue Thomiste* 56 (1956): 389-421. Fr. Bernard Lucien seems to take the same approach today in *Révélation et Tradition: Les lieux médiateurs de la Révélation divine publique, du dépôt de la foi au Magistère vivant de l'Église* [Revelation and Tradition: the mediating sources of public divine Revelation, from the deposit of the faith to the living Magisterium of the Church] (Brannay: Éditions Nuntiavit, 2009).

²⁸ Brunero Gherardini, *Quod et tradidi vobis: La tradizione, vita e giovinezza della Chiesa* (Frigento, AV: Casa Mariana Editrice, 2010), 71-96.

²⁹ Vatican Council II, Dogmatic Constitution *Dei Verbum*, 10.

The Magisterium is an instrument which the Church utilizes, and she is, in turn, the true subject-organ of Tradition. This is not a matter of subtleties. Today the doctrine of the theological sources is often forgotten: nevertheless, it would be an excellent tool with which to confront the contemporary religious crisis, which is expressed, among other ways, precisely in the contrast between the "new post-conciliar theology" and the "Magisterium."[30] What ought to be emphasized in opposition to the theologians of "dissent," instead of the "Magisterium," which they understand as an arbitrary exercise of authority, is the Catholic Sacred Tradition which includes, naturally, the unchangeable past and present Magisterium of the Church. Fifty years after the conclusion of Vatican Council II what has happened, instead, even in the minds of some neo-conciliar theologians,[31] is that the Magisterium tends to become the expression of authority that is an end in itself, as opposed to Tradition. Nobody speaks any more about the role of Tradition as the "*regula fidei*" [rule of faith], whereas the relation between Tradition and Magisterium is a central point that must be examined in greater depth.

6. What is Tradition?

Over the course of history the word Tradition has taken on many connotations that have falsified its first and truest meaning. Just think of the use that is made of it in Gnostic and esoteric circles, which cite an alleged "primordial Tradition" from which a syncretistic "transcendent unity of religions" is supposedly derived. The only Tradition of interest to us, though, is Tradition in the specific sense in which the Catholic Church intends it.[32]

Unlike any other tradition, the Church's has an origin and a precise content about which no ambiguity is possible. The Catholic

---

[30] *Cf.* for example the Instruction *Donum Veritatis* by the Congregation for the Doctrine of the Faith (May 24, 1990), in *AAS* 82 (1990): 1550-1570, which speaks explicitly about a "parallel Magisterium of the theologians" opposed to the Magisterium of the Pastors (no. 27).

[31] *Cf.* for example Fr. Pietro Cantoni, *Riforma nella continuità: Riflessioni sul Vaticano II e sull'anticonciliarismo* (Milan: Sugarco, 2011).

[32] There is a Tradition (which is recognized by the Church) that refers to the primordial Revelation, just as there is obviously a biblical Revelation which has its culmination in the coming of the Messiah and continues in the New Testament as the "New Covenant" in the redeeming Blood of Christ.

Tradition begins with the Church herself, when Jesus Christ, her Head and Founder, transmitted to His disciples a deposit of truths to spread, over the course of the centuries, to the farthest corners of the world.

These truths communicated by Jesus during His earthly life were spelled out, explained, and examined in depth in the 40 days that intervened between the Resurrection and His Ascension into Heaven. The Gospel does not tell us much about this period, but we know that He appeared several times to the apostles, performing miracles, like the miraculous catch on the Lake of Tiberias and the calling of Simon Peter which concludes the Gospel of St. John (Jn. 21:1-25). We can imagine the conversations that extended uninterruptedly during those days and how intimate, substantial, and fruitful they must have been for the souls of the disciples. He spoke to them about the Kingdom of God, sometimes explaining what He had said without being fully understood before His death; other times revealing mysteries and secrets relating to the sacraments and especially to the Holy Sacrifice of the Mass; still other times, clarifying for them the profound meaning of the Sacred Scriptures. Then He continually encouraged them, instilling peace and consolation in their hearts. Nor should we overlook the hidden mission of Our Lady, Mother of the Church, in reinforcing, sustaining, and clarifying the transmission of these truths during her earthly life. In the first 30 years of the Church's life, there was nothing but Tradition, in other words the testimony and the teaching of the apostles. Catholic Tradition therefore is nothing other than the teaching of Jesus transmitted to the apostles and handed down by them from generation to generation. The divine truth transmitted by Christ to the apostles and by the apostles to the Church is described by theologians as *traditio apostolica* or *depositum apostolicum*.[33] St. Paul refers to this Tradition, urging Timothy to be faithful to what he has received, which he himself will have to teach: "O Timothy, keep that which is committed to thy trust, avoiding the profane novelties of words and oppositions of knowledge falsely so called. Which some promising

---

[33] Thus, for example, Matthias Joseph Scheeben (1835-1888), *Handbuch der Dogmatik*, 4 vols. (Herder: Freiburg, 1873-1903), no. 203. [English edition: *Handbook of Catholic Dogmatics* 1.1 (Steubenville: Emmaus Academic, 2018).]

[*i.e.* For by professing it, some] have erred concerning the Faith" (1 Tim. 6:20-21).

Tradition includes not only a patrimony of truths but also a series of moral precepts, liturgical rules, and norms of ecclesiastical governance.[34] There is no more condensed expression of Tradition than the liturgy, in which faith and Tradition meet. The word *traditio*, in its original sense, refers to the transmission of the *symbola fidei*, which is to say those verbal formulas confirmed by the ecclesiastical authority that are designed for the public profession of the Faith. The *traditio* is expressed in the delivery of truths destined to form the *depositum fidei* [deposit of faith], but it is also an inquiry into the ways in which these truths are to be transmitted and an inquiry into the symbols and rituals that effectively express these truths. Indeed, every truth is translated in a liturgy, according to the well-known axiom of Prosper of Aquitaine, "*Lex orandi, lex credendi*" ["the law of prayer is the law of belief"] (or "*legem credendi lex statuat supplicandi*" ["the law of prayer establishes the law of belief"].[35]

The first Christians are presented to us as being united both in the doctrine of their Faith and in their worship: "They were persevering in the doctrine of the apostles and in the communication of the breaking of bread and in prayers" (Acts 2:42). St. Irenaeus wrote:

> The Church…although scattered throughout the whole world, carefully preserves this preaching and this Faith, as if occupying but one house. She also believes these points just as if she had but one soul, and one and the same heart, and she proclaims them, and teaches them, and hands them down, with perfect harmony, as if she possessed only one mouth. For, although the languages of the world are dissimilar, yet the import of the Tradition is one and the same.[36]

The "import of Tradition," according to St. Irenaeus, is therefore the continuity of the teaching of the apostles in the Church founded by them. All the Fathers of the Church agree on this point: Tradition is the apostolic teaching inasmuch as it has been transmitted by successive generations and has come down to us unchanged. In the patristic view, heresy is that which is "new" and detached from Tradition. The criterion of truth is based, according to the famous

---

[34] *Cf.* Henri Holstein, *La Tradizione nella Chiesa* (Milan: Vita e Pensiero, 1968), 53-54.

[35] Prosper of Aquitaine, *De vocatione omnium gentium*, 1, 12, in PL 51, 664CD.

[36] St. Irenaeus of Lyons, *Contra haereses*, I, 10, 2 (English translation based on ANF 1:331a).

formula of St. Vincent of Lerins, on that which is handed down and believed everywhere, always, and by all: *"quod ubique, quod semper, quod ab omnibus creditur."*[37] For the saint from Lerins, the mission of theology is to preserve the deposit according to St. Paul's prescription to Timothy:

> What is "The deposit"? That which has been entrusted to thee, not that which thou hast thyself devised: a matter not of wit, but of learning; not of private adoption, but of public tradition; a matter brought to thee, not put forth by thee, wherein thou art bound to be not an author but a keeper, not a teacher but a disciple, not a leader but a follower.[38]

Theological reflection on Tradition occurred above all after the rejection of it by the Protestant Revolution. In its Fourth Session, celebrated on April 8, 1546, the Council of Trent affirmed that the Gospel of Christ is contained "in the written books and unwritten traditions that have come down to us, having been received by the apostles from the mouth of Christ Himself or from the apostles by the dictation of the Holy Spirit, and have been transmitted, as it were, from hand to hand."[39]

Vatican Council I confirmed these definitions in almost identical words.[40] The great theologians of the Roman school developed these concepts. Cardinal Billot defines Tradition as "the rule of faith that is prior [earlier in time] to all the others," a rule of faith which is not only remote but also proximate and immediate, depending on the point of view from which it is presented to us.[41] Monsignor Brunero Gherardini, a brilliant contemporary representative of that school, proposes this definition of it: "Tradition is the official transmission of divine Revelation in the spatial-temporal dimension by the Church

---

[37] St. Vincent of Lerins, *Commonitorium*, II, 6 (NPNF-2 11:132b).
[38] St. Vincent of Lerins, *Commonitorium*, XXII, 53 (NPNF-2 11:147b).
[39] DH 1501.
[40] DH 3006.
[41] *Cf.* Cardinal Louis Billot, S.J., *De Immutabilitate traditionis* (1907), French translation by Fr. Jean-Michel Gleize, *Tradition et modernisme: De l'immuable tradition, contre la nouvelle hérésie de l'évolutionnisme* (Villegenon: Courrier de Rome, 2007), 32, 37.

and its organs that were divinely instituted for this purpose and are infallibly assisted by the Holy Ghost."[42]

7. Tradition and the Church

To the one objective sense of Tradition as the sacred deposit transmitted by the Church, the theologians of the 19th and 20th centuries added the sense of "subjective" and "active" Tradition.[43] Objective Tradition—that which is believed and transmitted—is the equivalent of the "*depositum Fidei.*" Subjective Tradition, which the theologians prefer to call "active," is the kind that refers to the act of transmission or to the subject himself who transmits it.[44] Some writers claim that this act coincides with the Church's Magisterium, but this is an improper identification. The Magisterium is, in fact, the Church's authority to teach. But Tradition is not only "taught" and "defined," it is also kept and believed: and although the act of teaching is reserved to the teaching Church alone, the act of believing and keeping belongs to the whole Church, teaching and learning. In this regard it would be reductive to describe the Magisterium as the sole voice or even as the exclusive proximate "rule" of Tradition. More precisely, Melchior Cano, but also, essentially, Scheeben and Franzelin, describe as the "organ" of Tradition not the Magisterium, but the subject "Church" in her totality, who performs her *munus* [duty, office] both through the Magisterium when she teaches, and through the "*sensus fidei*" when she believes: "The whole Church, the people of God in its entirety," Schmaus writes, "is the subject of oral Tradition, although not all the members exercise the same office."[45]

---

[42] Brunero Gherardini, *Quaecumque dixero vobis: Parola di Dio e Tradizione a confronto con la storia e la teologia* (Turin: Lindau, 2011), 170. "Within Tradition we distinguish between *divine Tradition* and *apostolic Tradition*; the latter is then subdivided into *constitutive Tradition*—which was concluded with the death of Christ and of the last apostle—and *continuative Tradition*—which is entrusted to the evangelizing mission of the Church" (*ibid.*, 176).

[43] See, for example, Michael Schmaus, *Dogmatica cattolica* (Casale Monferrato: Marietti, 1959), 1:98-99.

[44] In this sense, according to Albert Michel, "Tradition is the teaching communicated or else the act itself of communicating this teaching" (DTC, XV, 1, col. 1252). *Cf.* also Brunero Gherardini, *Quod et tradidi vobis*, 209.

[45] Michael Schmaus, *op. cit.*, 103.

The inseparable bond of apostolic succession ties the Church to Tradition. St. Irenaeus, for example, recalls the figure of St. Polycarp as follows:

> But Polycarp also was not only instructed by apostles, and conversed with many who had seen Christ, but was also, by apostles in Asia, appointed bishop of the Church in Smyrna, whom I also saw in my early youth, for he tarried [on earth] a very long time, and, when a very old man, gloriously and most nobly suffering martyrdom, departed this life, having always taught the things which he had learned from the apostles, and which the Church has handed down, and which alone are true. To these things all the Asiatic Churches testify, as do also those men who have succeeded Polycarp down to the present time.[46]

The Council of Trent, in defining Tradition, points outs apostolic character as a criterion of authenticity: "traditions that have come down to us…and have been transmitted, as it were, from hand to hand."[47] "The only true Tradition is the one that is based on apostolic Tradition," contemporary Roman theology repeats, along with Monsignor Gherardini.[48] This means that the Roman Pontiff, the successor of Peter, prince of the apostles, is the guarantor for the excellence of the Church's Tradition. But it also means that in no case can the object of the Faith exceed what is given to us by the testimonies of the apostles. "There is and there can be nothing *above and beyond* the apostolic experience, *above and beyond* the knowledge that they had from Christ."[49]

The Church does not recognize "novelties" but only the explanation, clarification, and definition of the traditions handed down by the Divine Master to the apostles. Ecclesiastical Tradition, which represents the verbal tradition of the apostles, is distinguished from every purely human tradition, because its organs, materially speaking, are not "the wise" or "the experts," but rather ecclesiastical authorities, and its organ in the formal sense is the Church herself.[50] This Tradition, although it is transmitted by men, is not purely human, but supernatural and therefore guaranteed by the Holy Ghost.

---

[46] St. Irenaeus of Lyons, *Adversus Haereses*, III, 3, 4 (ANF 1:417ab).
[47] DH 1501.
[48] Brunero Gherardini, *Quod et tradidi vobis*, 312.
[49] Henri Holstein, *op. cit.*, 242.
[50] Matthias Joseph Scheeben, *Dogmatics*, no. 309.

Scheeben writes that the principal representative of Tradition, although not the sole one, is the Roman Apostolic See. "The decisive and constant Tradition itself of the Roman Church," he explains, "can continue to exist and have its full validity, even though the individual pope does not give expression to it in all his acts or contradicts it in individual acts—but not in his judicial acts." He then adds in a note: "It was consequently extremely foolish and sacrilegious, with regard to the claim of infallibility of judgment, to attribute to Pius IX the remark: *'La tradizione sono io'* = 'I am Tradition.'"[51] The Church is not infallible because she exercises a form of authority, but rather because she transmits a doctrine.

Besides the Apostolic See, the center and principal channel of Tradition, there are secondary conductors and channels, which even though they do not represent Tradition from a juridical, official perspective, do represent it from a moral perspective.[52] The doctrine of the Fathers and Doctors of the Church, taught uniformly and constantly, is the very teaching of the Holy Ghost which is communicated and preserved in the Church through His supernatural influence.[53] To this should be added the consensus of the theologians and the liturgy, which because of its cultural nature can be described as a *protestatio fidei*, a "doxological" form of the profession of the Church's faith.[54]

8. The Church, the Mystical Body of Christ

The one, holy, catholic, and apostolic Church cannot be confined in rigid conceptual categories, because, as Cardinal Journet remarks, "she is too rich to be reduced to just one concept and to correspond to just one name."[55] Nevertheless, according to Pius XII, who wished to define and describe the Catholic Church, "we shall find nothing nobler, more sublime, or more divine than the expression 'the Mystical Body of Jesus Christ.'"[56]

---

[51] *Ibid.*, no. 337.
[52] *Ibid.*, no. 341.
[53] *Ibid.*, nos. 341, 372.
[54] Bernard Lucien, *op. cit.*, 236.
[55] Cardinal Charles Journet, *L'Église du Verbe Incarné*, 2 vols. (Paris: Desclée de Brouwer, 1941), 2:50.
[56] Pius XII, Encyclical *Mystici Corporis*, 13; *cf.* Rom 12:4-6; 1 Cor 12:12-27; Eph 4:4.

Since it is a Body, the visible Church constitutes, by the divine will, a society, or an organism composed of a great many human beings subject to one and the same authority and united by the bond of one and the same law.[57] It consists of a human element that is visible and external, namely the multitude of human beings who compose it, and of a divine element that is spiritual and invisible, namely the supernatural gifts that place the human society under the influence of the Holy Ghost, the soul and unitive principle of the whole organism.[58] Pius XII recalls the words of St. Paul: "As in one body we have many members, but all the members have not the same office, so we, being many, are one body in Christ; and every one members one of another" (Rom. 12:4-5).

The Church is not an egalitarian society in which all the members have equal duties and identical rights. Its constitution is hierarchical because the mandate to govern it was entrusted by Christ to Peter and the apostles, who have handed it down without interruption to their successors. In it we can distinguish the teaching Church and the learning Church, the former made up of the pastors and their head, who is the pope; the second made up of those who are subject to the legitimate pastors.

The Council of Trent, in its Decree on Holy Orders dated July 15, 1563, declares anathema anyone who says that "in the Catholic Church there is no hierarchy instituted by divine ordinance that consists of bishops, priests, and ministers."[59] The Holy Ghost, however, assists not only the teaching Church but the whole social organism, which forms "one body and one spirit," united by "one Lord, one Faith, one baptism" (Eph. 4:4-5). The error of those who wish to transfer the functions of the teaching Church to the learning Church is accompanied by the opposite error of those who would like to reduce the learning Church to a body that must follow the pastors mechanically and passively.

---

[57] Alfredo Ottaviani, *Institutiones Iuris Publici Ecclesiastici*, 2 vols. (Rome: Tipografia Poliglotta Vaticana, 1958-1960), 4th ed., 141-146; Alfons Maria Stickler, "Il mistero della Chiesa nel Diritto canonico," in Various Authors, *Il mistero della Chiesa* (Rome: Paoline, 1962), 166-181; Javier Hervada, *Elementos de Derecho constitucional canónico* (Pamplona: Eunsa, 1987), 170-174.

[58] Pius XII, Encyclical *Mystici Corporis*, 40, 64-65.

[59] DH nos. 1776, 1768.

9. The authority of the Magisterium

The apostolic hierarchy in the Church exercises two powers mysteriously united in the same person: the power of order and the power of jurisdiction.[60] The distinction between sacramental power and the power of jurisdiction is clearly stated by St. Thomas[61] and is, as Scheeben observes, profound and has a wealth of important consequences.[62] Both powers are directed to accomplish the particular purposes of the Church, but each with its own characteristics that distinguish it profoundly from the other: the *potestas ordinis* is the power to distribute the means of the divine grace and refers to the administration of the sacraments and the conducting of official worship; the *potestas iurisdictionis* is the power to govern the ecclesiastical institution and the individual faithful.[63]

The Magisterium is that part of the power of jurisdiction which consists of the Church's right and duty to teach all nations the doctrine of the Gospel according to the mandate of its Founder.[64] From its beginning, indeed, the Church has claimed as its privilege the full possession of the truth and, as its mandatory duty, the task of proclaiming it to mankind. This is its *ministerium verbi* (Acts 6:1-7).

The traditional doctrine maintains that the Magisterium is not an independent power, but that it must be included in the power of jurisdiction. This is how reliable canonists put it, from Fathers Wernz and Vidal to Cardinal Stickler, along with renowned theologians, from Scheeben to Cardinal Journet.[65] Scheeben rightly notes that the old scholastic-canonical division *potestas ordinis* and *potestas*

---

[60] Pius X, Encyclical *Ad sinarum gentem* (October 7, 1954), in *Discorsi e Radiomessaggi*, XVI, p. 404; Felix M. Cappello, S.J., *Summa Iuris Publici Ecclesiastici* (Rome: Pontificiae Universitatis Gregorianae, 1954), 6th ed., 116-117; Pietro Gasparri, *Institutiones Iuris Publici* (Milan: Giuffré, 1992), 203-204; Alfredo Ottaviani, *op. cit.*, I: *Ecclesiae Constitutio Socialis et Potestas*, 178-185; Don Dario Composta, *La Chiesa visibile* (Vatican City: LEV, 2010).

[61] St. Thomas Aquinas, *Summa theologiae* II-II, q. 39, art. 3, resp.; III, q. 6, art. 2.

[62] Matthias J. Scheeben, *I misteri del cristianesimo*, Italian translation (Brescia: Morcelliana, 1960), 3rd ed., 405.

[63] Charles Journet, *L'Église du Verbe Incarné*, 1:31; Felix M. Cappello, S.J., *Summa Iuris, op. cit.*, 284; Alfredo Ottaviani, *Institutiones, op. cit.*, 123.

[64] Ferdinand Claeys-Boùùaert, "Magistère ecclésiastique," in DDC, VI, col. 694.

[65] Franciscus X. Wernz, S.J. and Petrus Vidal, S.J., *Ius canonicum* (Rome: Gregoriana, 1943), 2:52; Alfons Maria Stickler, "Le pouvoir de gouvernement, pouvoir ordinaire et pouvoir délégué," in: *L'Année Canonique*, 24 (1980): 69-84; Matthias J. Scheeben, *Dogmatik, op. cit.*; Charles Journet, *op. cit.*

iurisdictionis is the only formally correct one.[66] In fact, the Magisterium, "considered concretely and as inseparably united to the power to command obedience to the Faith, is not adequately distinguished from the power of jurisdiction; for this reason the common usage recognizes only these two major divisions of ecclesiastical power, in other words, the power of order and the power of jurisdiction."[67] This is demonstrated by the exercise of jurisdiction by prelates who do not have the fullness of the power of order, as was the case with some popes who, although not bishops at the time of their election, exercised jurisdiction even before being consecrated bishops.

Not until the 19th century did theologians and, above all, German canonists introduce a *potestas magisterii* alongside the *potestas ministerii* and the *potestas iurisdictionis*,[68] under the Protestant influence of that "primacy of the word," which, according to Reformed Christians, belongs to the baptized without exception.[69] The new tripartite division: Order, Magisterium, Jurisdiction, seems to have been accepted by Vatican Council II, when, in the Constitution *Lumen Gentium*, it distinguishes three different functions within the Church: the *munus sanctificandi,* the *munus docendi* and the *munus regendi*. This division, adopted also by some conservative theologians, has a relative value, though, responding more than anything to practical and descriptive needs.[70]

10. Tradition and the Magisterium

Therefore, we must not confuse the Magisterium, understood as the exercise of a power belonging to the sphere of jurisdiction, with the subject that exercises it, the Church, and with its object, the

---

[66] Matthias J. Scheeben, *Dogmatik*, no. 111.
[67] J. Baucher, "Juridiction," in DTC, 8/2, col. 1977. This principle was applied also in the old Code of Canon Law, in which the term *potestas magisterii* was never used; furthermore the Magisterium itself appears as an office belonging to the power of jurisdiction (Vincenzo Politi, *La giurisdizione ecclesiastica e la sua delegazione* [Milan: La Tradizione Editrice, 1937], 26). In the sacramental context, the new Code of Canon Law replaces the term *potestas* with *facultas* (Eugenio Corecco, *Théologie et droit canon* [Fribourg: Éditions Universitaires, 1990], 285-287).
[68] D. Le Tourneau, *op. cit.*, 275; Yves Congar, *op. cit.*, 94-95.
[69] Brunero Gherardini, *Creatura Verbi: La Chiesa nella teologia di Martin Lutero* (Rome: VivereIn, 1994), 231-278.
[70] Klaus Mörsdorf, "Munus regendi e potestas iurisdictionis," in *Schriften zum Kanonischen Recht* (Padeborn: Schöningh, 1989), 216-218.

depositum fidei et morum, the treasure of faith and morals entrusted by Christ to the Church.

If the Magisterium refers, above all, to the authority which over the centuries has guaranteed the objective truth that is handed down, then the Magisterium tends to be identified with the Church or, more precisely, with the physical or moral persons who hold its offices: the pope or the bishops;[71] in this sense, some have spoken about the Magisterium as the "proximate rule" of faith. Tradition, however, cannot be identified with the current preaching of the Church, nor can the Magisterium constitute the only and immediate rule of faith.

Since the Magisterium is the Church's power to teach, it is distinguished from Tradition, because it is founded on objective Tradition and depends on the "active" Tradition, which is the Church. The Magisterium is not Tradition, because it receives it and it is exercised in order to guarantee it. If it identified itself with Tradition, it could "create" Tradition or otherwise "increase" Revelation, instead of limiting itself to receiving and transmitting it. For this reason Fr. Holstein writes that: "The Magisterium is not the Tradition, it does not create it, nor does it change it, but it discerns and expresses it."[72]

The Magisterium is not the Church, either, because it constitutes one of its functions and is exercised by the Church to teach revealed Truths. The unification of the three subjects—Tradition, Church, Magisterium—that the Constitution *Dei Verbum* of Vatican Council II seems to propose, creates serious confusion, even though the conciliar Constitution specifies, in no.10, that: "This Magisterium is not superior to the Word of God, but is its servant. It teaches only what has been handed on to it. At the divine command and with the help of the Holy Spirit, it listens to this devotedly, guards it with dedication and expounds it faithfully."[73]

11. The criterion of Tradition

Someone may ask the question: who interprets Tradition? The question is improper, since Tradition is above all the *regula fidei*, thus the criterion and not an object of interpretation. But starting from

---

[71] See for example J.-V. Bainvel, *op. cit.*, and the article "Tradition" by A. Michel in DTC, 15/1, col. 1252.
[72] Henri Holstein, *op. cit.*, 128.
[73] Vatican Council II, Dogmatic Constitution *Dei Verbum*, no. 10.

Luther and Descartes, a kind of subjectivism unknown to the Fathers of the Church, to Scholasticism and to the great theologians of the Counter-Reformation made its way even into Catholic thought. The attention until then reserved to the objectivity of the things known was shifted to the activity of the knowing subject. In theological knowledge, this cognitive process led to the primacy of epistemology and later of "hermeneutics."[74] Today, interpretation tends to become a hermeneutical judgment, and knowing "who" interprets has become more important than knowing "what" is interpreted. We are faced with the "hermeneutic of the subject" that is typical of modern and post-modern thought, in which the knowing subject predominates over the objective data to be known. There is also an equivocation in the primary use of the term "interpret" as compared with the terms keep and transmit. In fact, Tradition, like any other truth, should not be "interpreted" but, if necessary, clarified and defined and, first of all, received and transmitted.

Therefore the correct question is: who transmits Tradition? And the answer can only be: the teaching Church and the learning Church, in its entirety. The learning Church is limited to receiving it, believing it and retransmitting it; the teaching Church, above all in the person of the pope, proclaims it, defines it, teaches it. But the fact that the Church transmits Tradition does not mean it can "interpret" it to the point of denying or contradicting it.

It is a different question to ask: Who exercises the Magisterium (or else: who "teaches") within the Church? The answer this time can only be: the pope and the bishops who make up the teaching Church. But the learning Church, while having no power of Magisterium, is also assisted by the Holy Spirit. In this sense, Melchior Cano states that "not only the universal Church, that is, the whole of all the faithful, has this eternal Spirit of Truth, but the princes and the pastors of the Church have it too."[75]

The hermeneutic of the subject ("who" interprets rather than "what" is transmitted) also runs the risk of triggering an endless hermeneutical chain. This means, as Fr. Cavalcoli warns, that "every interpretation, no matter how clear, must be 'interpreted'; but the

---

[74] See for example Gilles Routhier and Guy Jobin, *L'Autorité et les Autorités: L'herméneutique théologique de Vatican II* (Paris: Cerf, 2010).

[75] Melchior Cano, *op. cit.*, 250.

interpretation too must be interpreted: and so on to infinity, without ever reaching a definitive explanation or clarification."[76] If Tradition needs to be interpreted by the Magisterium, we should ask who interprets the Magisterium. And if the pope is the interpreter of the Magisterium, we should then wonder who interprets the pope, because there would no longer be an interpretation that was objective and definitive in itself. Moreover, those who say that the pope is the rule of interpreting Tradition are forced to affirm that the pope's speeches need an appropriate exegesis. Often, those who proclaim "*Tu es Petrus*" are referring not to the Roman Pontiff but to themselves…

There is no more equivocal formula than the one which claims that the Magisterium interprets Tradition. Indeed, the term Tradition is then understood as objective teaching that is limited to the past; the term Magisterium is, on the contrary, understood in a subjective sense, identifying it with the teaching authority that speaks in the present. This current Magisterium, defined as "living," becomes the source of the objective Magisterium, and the "living" Magisterium becomes, in turn, the hermeneutical rule of Tradition, as if that were not a perennial, living Magisterium. The emphasis is shifted from the objective transmitted teaching to the subject who transmits the received teaching.[77] In reality, as we have seen, the Magisterium is nothing but a power which is used by the subject "Church" to carry out its duty to "teach" the faithful and it cannot be considered in any way a *locus theologicus* that is autonomous and independent in itself.

In what way can we say that there is no Tradition without the Magisterium of the Church? In the sense that in order to become part of Tradition a truth must be taught by the Church and taught not only once, but constantly and consistently; once this truth is part of the Tradition it cannot be changed by the subsequent Magisterium of the Church. In this sense it is through the Church and its Magisterium that Revelation becomes Tradition.[78]

The Magisterium of the Church, that is, the act with which the teaching Church exercises its right/duty to teach, is necessary in

---

[76] Giovanni Cavalcoli, O. P., *La questione dell'eresia oggi* (Rome: VivereIn, 2008), 134, 284.
[77] Brunero Gherardini, *Quaecumque dixero vobis, op. cit.*, 159.
[78] *Ibid.*, 38.

order for a certain religious or moral trucarth to become part of the Tradition of the Church. In this respect, there is no Tradition without the Magisterium. But the Magisterium, in turn, is nourished by the Tradition, which it preserves and transmits: it depends on it, it cannot create it, but must receive it; it can apply it to the new questions that emerge in history, as it happened with the moral problems of contraception and in-vitro fertilization. But the objective criterion, the rule of faith, is the truth taught and transmitted by the Magisterium, not the Magisterium in itself.

In descending order of importance, Tradition is first, then the Church and after that the Magisterium, which is a "power" that the Church exercises to perpetuate the Tradition. The Magisterium, in itself, is not a "source," but a "*potestas*," and can in no way take advantage of Tradition. The legitimate authority of the Church can exercise its power badly, since its infallibility is granted only under certain conditions. In case of doubt, it will be necessary to refer to the "*depositum fidei*" that the Church preserves, to the Tradition of which it is organ and voice. No one else, except the teaching Church, can define the truths of faith, but the *sensus fidei* of the faithful is sufficient to know and to preserve these truths.

The Magisterium of the Church is not the fruit of the defining will of the pope and the bishops; rather it depends on the sources of Revelation—Scripture and Tradition—and cannot be separated from them. Before the Magisterium there is the Church, before the Church there is Tradition, before Tradition there is the Revelation, and before Revelation there is the Revelator, who is Christ Himself. Jesus Christ-God transmits His divine Word to the Church, so that it can preserve it and re-transmit it over the centuries; Tradition is the way in which Revelation is transmitted, but it is also the content or, if you prefer, the container of Revelation. In this sense, as Benedict XVI reiterated, "with the Church's living Tradition, [Scripture] constitutes the supreme rule of faith."[79]

---

[79] Benedict XVI, Post-Synodal Apostolic Exhortation *Verbum Domini* (September 30, 2010), in: http://w2.vatican.va/content/benedict-xvi/en/apost_exhortations/documents/hf_ben-xvi_exh_20100930_verbum-domini.html

12. Teaching Church and learning Church

Tradition certainly needs organs: among these organs, the first one is the Church. However, not by chance, Fr. Melchior Cano distinguishes between the Church as a whole and the Councils and the pope. The teaching Church, of which the Councils and, *in primis*, the pope are the supreme expression, is a part, albeit the most eminent, of the Church, which is nonetheless a larger organism, comprising also the learning Church. Melchior Cano, and with him Fathers Perrone, Franzelin, Scheeben and most theologians, maintain that although only the teaching Church has the duty to teach and define, even the learning Church has the duty to preserve and transmit the *depositum fidei*. The whole 12th thesis of the treatise *De divina Traditione* by Franzelin is dedicated to showing "how the agreement of the faithful on the truths of faith is a criterion of the divine tradition."[80] The Church as a whole, and not just the teaching Church, is a "*locus theologicus*" and can be considered, before Councils and the pope, the authentic "organ" of Tradition.

The basic distinction between the teaching Church and the learning Church must be reaffirmed. The former is composed of those who have the *munus docendi*: the duty and the mission to teach. The latter is made up of the whole Church that receives the teaching of its pastors. Only the teaching Church has the right to make explicit the truths implicitly contained in the doctrine that it transmits, in the sense that it is the teaching Church that extracts, from the received heritage, implicit truths which it then makes explicit. But once these truths are made explicit by the extraordinary and infallible Magisterium, or by the ordinary and universal Magisterium, these truths belong to the whole Church, both teaching and learning, and no pope or Council has the authority to modify them in any way. For example: only the teaching Church had the power to define the dogma of the Immaculate Conception, which was freely discussed until 1854, but after its definition the dogma become part of the heritage of truths infallibly preserved by the learning Church also. At this point, not even the pope could deny this dogma: if he did so, he would fall into heresy.

---

[80] Cardinal Jean-Baptiste Franzelin, *De divina Traditione et Scriptura* (1870), French translation annotated and edited by Fr. J.-M. Gleize, *La Tradition* (Condé sur Noireau: Courrier de Rome, 2009), 139-195.

The Church has the mission of preserving, preaching and re-transmitting, integrally and faithfully until the end of time, the doctrine received from Christ Himself. This doctrine is preserved and re-transmitted by the whole Church, including the learning Church, but only the teaching Church can pronounce definitively on matters of faith and morals. No member of the learning Church, whether an individual or a community, has the authority to define controversial matters or to judge other brothers in faith.

13. The active and passive infallibility of the Church

The validity of the definitions of the teaching Church is in proportion to the authority that it attributes to itself at the moment when it intervenes. The maximum degree is infallibility. We must not confuse the infallibility of the Church with its indefectibility. Indefectibility is the guarantee that the Church has from its Founder to remain true to its identity until the end of time, in other words, to persevere, thanks to the assistance of the Holy Spirit, "*Spirit of Truth*" (Jn. 14:17), in its profession of the same Faith, of the same sacraments, of the same apostolic succession of government. Instead, infallibility is the prerogative whereby the Church and the pope, thanks to a special divine assistance, cannot err in defending and defining revealed doctrine. This supernatural prerogative is expressed in an extraordinary way when the pope pronounces *ex cathedra* with a judgment that is manifestly definitive and destined for the whole Church,[81] or in an ordinary way, when the pope and the bishops teach a doctrine continuously. But besides the infallibility of the teaching Church, exercised in the ordinary or extraordinary Magisterium, there is also an infallibility of the learning Church in believing these same truths. St. Thomas Aquinas refers to the infallibility of the Church as a whole when

---

[81] Federico dell'Addolorata, "Infallibilità," in EC, V, coll. 1920-1924. "Infallibility in the pope is a personal prerogative, not because as a private person he is safeguarded from error or from heresy (an open question) but in the sense that each of the successors of Peter without exception is infallible, and not just the series of them, or the Roman See, considered as a moral entity, as some Gallicans claim" (*ibid.*, col. 1923).

he states: "It is impossible for the judgment of the universal Church to be wrong in what pertains to the Faith."[82]

This means that both the *corpus docendi*, invested with the power to teach the whole Church, and the faithful generally in their belief, cannot fall into error. Of course this must not be understood in the sense of attributing a teaching role to the laity, as the progressive theologians claim,[83] but rather in the sense of acknowledging the role of the faithful in witnessing to what is taught them by the Tradition.

According to theologians, the learning Church is a subject of passive infallibility, the teaching Church—of active infallibility; however, the cause and means of the infallibility that is found in the learning Church is the teaching Church, because it is the one to which the charisma of infallibility is directly promised. To the learning Church, as a body of believers, belong not only the faithful, but also the priests themselves, the bishops, and the pope, since all are bound to believe the truths revealed by God, the superiors no less than the inferiors. In the Church, there is only one infallibility, in which all its members participate in an organic and differentiated way: each according to his own ecclesiastical office. Individual Christians can err in matters of faith, even when they hold the highest ecclesiastical offices, but the Church as such cannot. In this sense, as St. Thomas Aquinas declares, the Church as *universitas fidelium* cannot err.[84]

14. The Christian sense of faith

Therefore, according to correct theology, the organ of Tradition is not only the authority of the Church when it exercises its Magisterium, but also the *sensus fidei* of the Catholic people.[85]

---

[82] St. Thomas Aquinas, *Quodlibet* 9, q. 8, art. 1.
[83] On the argument claiming a "magisterial" role of the faithful, see for example the special issue of *Concilium* 21/4 (1985): 7-124, dedicated to "The Doctrinal Authority of the Faithful."
[84] St. Thomas Aquinas, *Summa theologiae*, II-II, q. 1, art. 9.
[85] Cf. Jesús Sancho Bielsa, *Infalibilidad del pueblo de Dios: "Sensus fidei" e infalibilidad orgánica de la Iglesia en la constitución "Lumen Gentium" del Concilio Vaticano II* (Pamplona: Universidad de Navarra, 1979), 282-284; Dario Vitali, *Sensus fidelium: Una funzione ecclesiale di intelligenza della fede* (Brescia: Morcelliana, 1993); Christoph Ohly, *Sensus fidei fidelium* (St. Ottilien: EOS Verlag, 1999).

The doctrinal infallibility of the teaching Church in union with the successors of Peter, has as its counterpart the creedal infallibility of the learning Church, based on the *sense of faith*, which the theologians Ocáriz and Blanco explain as

> the ability of the believer, not only to believe what it is presented to him by the Church as truths of faith, but also and above all the capacity to distinguish, as though instinctively, what is in harmony with the Faith from what is not, and also the ability to draw the profounder consequences from the truths taught by the Magisterium, not by theological reasoning, but spontaneously, through a sort of knowledge by connaturality. In fact, the virtue of faith (*habitus fidei*) produces a connaturality of the human mind with the revealed mysteries, which works in such a way that the supernatural truth attracts the intellect.[86]

Faith is not the product of mere reasoning, but intuition of the divine truth, "the proof of things not seen" according to an expression of Benedict XVI.[87] The doctrine of knowledge *per modum inclinationis* or *per quandam connaturalitatem*[88] is a form of interior understanding that springs from faith as *instinctus* or *lumen fidei*: "*lumen fidei*—St. Thomas writes—*facit videre ea quae creduntur*"[89]: the light of faith shows us what must be believed. "Just as through the other habits of virtue the individual knows what is appropriate for him in accordance with that habit, so too through the habit of faith the human mind is urged to give assent to those (doctrines) which are in keeping with the true Faith and not to others."[90]

For St. Bonaventure, too, wisdom is the knowledge of higher causes, not so much in a speculative and intellectual way, but rather through a certain inclination and connaturality that God infuses in our hearts.[91] The sense of faith that the believer receives from Christ is the supernatural ability he has to perceive, discern, penetrate and apply revealed truth in his life, under the influence of the Holy Spir-

---

[86] Fernando Ocáriz and Antonio Blanco, *Rivelazione, fede e credibilità: Corso di teologia fondamentale* (Rome: Edizioni Università della Santa Croce, 2001), 84.

[87] Benedict XVI, Encyclical *Spe Salvi* (November 30, 2007), no. 7.

[88] *Cf.* St. Thomas Aquinas, *Summa theologiae*, II-II, q. 45, art. 2. See also: José Miguel Pero-Sanz, *El conocimiento por connaturalidad* (Pamplona: Eunsa, 1964).

[89] St. Thomas Aquinas, *Summa theologiae*, II-II, q. 1, art. 4 ad 3.

[90] *Ibid.*, II-II, q. 2, art. 3 ad 2.

[91] St. Bonaventure, *De perfectione evangelica*, q. 1, in *Opera omnia* (Ad Claras Aquas: Quaracchi, 1882-1902), 5:120.

it.⁹² Otherwise, one could not explain how simple folk and the illiterate are sometimes more enlightened and rooted in faith than the theologians themselves.

This sense of faith exists in all believers, including sinners, even if those who are in God's grace have a deeper and more intense knowledge of the dogmas of Faith than someone who is in sin; and among those who are in God's grace insight is proportional to the degree of sanctity. In fact, this insight is an illumination that comes from the grace of faith and from the gifts of the Holy Spirit in the soul, especially those of understanding, knowledge and wisdom.⁹³

It is no wonder then that the Fathers of the Church, the theologians and, above all, the various Councils and the successors of Peter, when speaking about the knowledge of the revealed deposit, mention that "*gift of the Holy Spirit*" which is the common privilege to all members of the Church.

An eminent Franciscan theologian, Fr. Carlo Balić, calls it "Catholic common sense" or "Christian sense" (*sensus christianus*), or "sense of faith" (*sensus fidei*).⁹⁴ Thanks to it the faithful perceive the truths preserved in the revealed deposit. In this way St. John's promise is fulfilled: "You have the unction [anointing] from the Holy One and know all things" (1 Jn. 2:20).

Ordinary common sense is the intelligence and ordinary light with which men are normally gifted: a quality which allows them to grasp the notions of good and evil, truth and falsehood, beauty and ugliness.⁹⁵ Supernatural or "Catholic common sense" is natural reason enlightened by the grace of the Holy Spirit, which every Christian receives with Baptism and Confirmation. These Sacraments infuse into us the *sensus fidei*, which is the adherence to the truths of Faith by supernatural instinct, even prior to theological reasoning. In the same way that common sense is measured by the objectivity of reality, subjective faith is measured by the objective

---

⁹² Jesús Sancho Bielsa, *op. cit.*, 256.
⁹³ Tommaso M. Bartolomei, "Natura, realtà, genesi e valore del 'Sensus fidei' nell'esplicitazione delle virtualità dei dogmi," in *Aprenas* 10/2 (luglio-settembre 1963), 268-294 at 270.
⁹⁴ Carlo Balić, O.F.M., "Il senso cristiano e il progresso del dogma," in *Gregorianum* 33/1 (1952): 106.-134 at 112-113.
⁹⁵ Réginald Garrigou-Lagrange, O.P., *Le sens commun: la philosophie de l'être et les formules dogmatiques* (Paris: Nouvelle Librairie Nationale, 1922).

rule of the supernatural truths contained in Tradition.⁹⁶ This Christian sense has nothing to do with the modernist religious sentiment condemned in the Encyclical *Pascendi* by St. Pius X, and even less with that *facultas appetendi et affectandi* [faculty of desiring and pursuing] mentioned in the Encyclical *Humani Generis* by Pius XII. In fact, the *sensus fidei* is not produced by sensitivity, but by faith, grace and the gifts of the Holy Spirit which illuminate the intellect and move the will.⁹⁷

"Now," Fr. Bali writes, "this Spirit of the seven gifts that dwells in us, not as in the midst of ruins, but as in a temple (1 Cor. 3:16-17; 6:19), is the spirit of Pentecost, the spirit of truth (Jn. 14:17) whose special mission is to reveal to the world the full substance of Christ and all the wonders that the Son of God had kept hidden or had not revealed completely and clearly."⁹⁸

15. *Sensus fidei* and Tradition

The Church's Magisterium is the responsibility only of those who, by Christ's will, have the right and office to teach: the apostles and their successors. The mass of the faithful has no part in this official teaching which they are limited to receive. "However," Fr. Bali writes, "one would be mistaken if he thought that this mass of the faithful lives in a merely passive and mechanical state with regard to this doctrine. In fact, the Faith of the faithful, like the teaching of the pastors, is under the influence of the Holy Spirit, and the faithful, through their Christian sense and their profession of faith, help to expound, publish, manifest and witness to Christian truth."⁹⁹

Although the faithful do not have the mission to teach, they do have the office of preserving and spreading their Faith. Even the great theologians of the Roman school, like Perrone, Scheeben and Franzelin, emphasize the role of the Holy Spirit in forming and main-

---

⁹⁶ In this sense, the principle of non-contradiction is one criterion for verifying the act of faith, just like any intellectual act (J.-M. Gleize, "Magistère et foi," in *Courrier de Rome* 344 (2011): 3).
⁹⁷ Carlo Balić, O.F.M., "Il senso cristiano," 113-114.
⁹⁸ *Ibid.*, 110.
⁹⁹ *Ibid.*, 125-126.

taining the *conscentia fidei communis* of the Christian people.[100] In particular, Cardinal Franzelin emphasizes the role of the Holy Spirit in preserving the faith of the learning Church and, like Melchior Cano, deems the *sensus fidelium* to be one of the organs of Tradition, of which it is a faithful echo. The *sensus fidelium*, witnessing to a doctrine as revealed, can be understood, in this sense, as a criterion of divine Revelation.

"The infallibility of the '*sensus fidei*,' manifested by the '*consensus fidelium*,'" Fathers Ocáriz and Blanco write, citing Franzelin, "exists even when it refers to truths not yet infallibly taught by the Magisterium. In this case the '*consensus fidelium*' is a sure criterion of truth because it is a criterion '*divinae traditionis*,'"[101] *sub ductu magisterii*, under the control of the Magisterium.

Therefore, the *sensus fidei* has value as a criterion, obviously always in relation to Tradition, on which it depends. From the doctrine of Cano and of the other above-cited authors it can be noted that the *sensus fidelium* constitutes a true and proper *locus theologicus*, a positive and sure criterion for determining whether a truth belongs to the domain of Tradition. This does not mean in any way that dogmatic truth should be the result of the feelings of the faithful and that nothing can be defined without first hearing the opinion of the universal Church, as if the Magisterium were just a revelator of the faith of the people and, so to speak, regulated by it in its magisterial function.[102] It means though that the Church's Magisterium cannot infallibly propose anything that is not contained at least implicitly in Tradition, which is the supreme rule of faith of the Church. This Tradition, the life and conscience of the Church's faith, is manifested in the *sensus fidei* not only of the pastors, but also of the Church Fathers, the Doctors, the Theologians and the simple faithful.

Vatican Council II confirmed this truth: the *consensus fidelium* or *communis fidelium consensus* is one of the organs of Tradition

---

[100] Cf. Franzelin, *De divina Traditione*, theses XI and XII; Matthias J. Scheeben, *Dogmatik*, no. 91 ff and no. 151 ff.; Walter Kasper, *Die Lehre von der Tradition in der Römischen Schule* (Freiburg: Herder, 1962), esp. 94-102.

[101] F. Ocáriz and A. Blanco, *op. cit.*, 85.

[102] The Decree *Lamentabili*, no. 6, condemns the Modernist proposition that "the 'Church learning' and the 'Church teaching' collaborate in such a way in defining truths that it only remains for the 'Church teaching' to sanction the opinions of the 'Church learning'" (Denzinger-Hünermann, no. 3406).

that expresses the Catholic Faith. For this reason all the faithful are obliged not only to profess their Faith interiorly, but also to manifest it outwardly. Chapter XII of *Lumen Gentium* states in this regard:

> The whole body of the faithful who have an anointing that comes from the Holy One, (*cf.* Jude 2:20 and 27), cannot err in matters of belief. This characteristic is shown in the supernatural appreciation of the faith of the whole people, when "from the bishops to the last of the faithful" they manifest a universal consent in matters of faith and morals. By this appreciation of the faith, aroused and sustained by the Spirit of truth, the People of God, guided by the sacred teaching authority (*magisterium*), and obeying it, receives not the mere word of men, but truly the word of God (*cf.* 1 Thess 2:13), the faith once for all delivered to the saints (see Jude 3), The People unfailingly adheres to this faith, penetrates it more deeply with right judgment, and applies it more fully in daily life.

Progressive authors have sometimes used this passage to challenge ecclesiastical authority, but this does not mean that it is false and that it cannot be understood, like many other passages of the Council, in accordance with Tradition.

Tradition is maintained and transmitted by the Church not only through the Magisterium, but by all the faithful, "from the bishops to the last of the lay faithful"[103] as expressed in the famous formula by St. Augustine, cited in the *Lumen Gentium*, no. 12. The doctor from Hippo in particular appeals to the "people of the faithful"[104] which does not exercise teaching authority , but, based on its *sensus fidei*, guarantees the continuity of the transmission of a truth. Over the course of history this role was played also by simple lay people: it is enough to recall, among the modern ones, Joseph de Maistre's contribution to the affirmation of the Roman primacy[105] and the defense of the Church by great authors such as

---

[103] St. Augustine, *De Praedestinatione sanctorum* 14, 27 (PL 44, 980).

[104] *Idem, Contra secundam Iuliani responsionem imperfectum opus*, cited in Italian from: *Polemica con Giuliano* II/1 (Rome: Città Nuova, 1993), 203-205.

[105] See his masterpiece *Du Pape* (Lyons: Rusard, 1819). About him see C. Constantin, in DTC, 9/2, cols. 1663-1678.

Louis Veuillot and Juan Donoso Cortés[106] in the 19th century and Plinio Corrêa de Oliveira[107] in the 20th.

Benedict XVI recalls the role of the *sensus fidei* with these words:

> Concerning the teaching on the Immaculate Conception, important theologians like Duns Scotus enriched what the People of God already spontaneously believed about the Blessed Virgin and expressed in acts of devotion, in the arts and in Christian life in general with the specific contribution of their thought…this is all thanks to that supernatural *sensus fidei*, namely, that capacity infused by the Holy Spirit that qualifies us to embrace the reality of the faith with humility of heart and mind…May theologians always be ready to listen to this source of faith and retain the humility and simplicity of children! I mentioned this a few months ago saying: "There have been great scholars, great experts, great theologians, teachers of faith who have taught us many things. They have gone into the details of Sacred Scripture…but have been unable to see the mystery itself, its central nucleus…The essential has remained hidden!…On the other hand, in our time there have also been 'little ones' who have understood this mystery. Let us think of St Bernadette Soubirous; of St. Thérèse of Lisieux, with her new interpretation of the Bible that is 'non-scientific' but goes to the heart of sacred Scripture." (*Homily, Mass for the Members of the International Theological Commission*, Pauline Chapel, Vatican City, 1 December 2009).[108]

The field in which the influence of the Holy Spirit on the faithful has been manifested most strongly in Church history was the veneration of the Blessed Virgin Mary. Thus, even before the Council of Ephesus proclaimed the Virgin Mary as the Mother of God,[109] St. Cyril[110] and St. Celestine[111] affirm that the Christian people already recognized the belief in the Divine Motherhood, as "the faith professed by the Universal Church."[112] For the same reasons the faithful people believed in the truth of the Immaculate Conception

---

[106] Juan Donoso Cortés, like Louis Veuillot, was consulted by Pius IX for the proclamation of the Immaculate Conception. Cf. his Letter to Cardinal Fornari dated June 19, 1852, in *Obras completas*, ed. by Carlos Valverde (Madrid: BAC, 1970), 2:744-761.

[107] On this author see Roberto de Mattei, *Il crociato del XX secolo* (Casale Monferrato: Piemme, 1996).

[108] Benedict XVI, General Audience, 7 July 2010.

[109] T. M. Bartolomei, "L'influsso del 'Senso della Fede,'" *op. cit.*, 284-285.

[110] St. Cyril, *Epist. IV ad Nestori* (PG 77, 47-50); *Epist. II ad Celestinum* (PG 77, 84).

[111] St. Celestine, *Epist. XII ad Cyrillum* (PG 77, 92-99).

[112] *Ibid.*, coll. 92-93.

and the Assumption. St. Alphonsus Liguori, in *The Glories of Mary*, puts the Immaculate Conception and the Assumption on the same level, because of the universality of the sense of faith. To prove the principle that the Church cannot err in what it believes, Cano cites the example of the truth of the Immaculate Conception and states: if the Universal Church supports this truth, it must be revealed. If that were not the case, the error about the faith of the Church would have to be attributed to Christ Himself who, as Head, moves and directs the Church, His Body.

For this reason, too, the Popes Pius IX and Pius XII, before the definition of the dogmas of the Immaculate Conception and of the bodily Assumption of the Blessed Virgin Mary, decided to consult the bishops throughout the world, who, besides expressing their own faith, had to give testimony also about the devotion of their faithful.[113]

Kneeling before the Blessed Sacrament and rejecting Communion in the hand, believing in the mediation of the Virgin Mary and in the assistance of the angels and saints, defending the kingship of Christ over human society, proclaiming with the Creed the uniqueness of the Catholic Church, outside of which there is no salvation: all this is nourished and born from the *sensus fidei* of the baptized.

16. *Sensus fidei* and resistance to the ecclesiastical authorities

According to the Dominican theologian García Extremeño, the *sensus fidei*, regarding the Magisterium, can: 1) *orient* it when it is a matter of disputed truths or when opinions are divided; 2) *awaken* the sense of pastors regarding truths that they perhaps have not considered correctly; 3) *replace* sometimes other arguments so as to proceed to the solemn definition of a truth maintained by the consent of the faithful.[114] However, the common sense of the faithful must: 1) *submit* to the judgment of the Magisterium; 2) *accept*

---

[113] *Cf.* Pius IX, Apostolic Letter *Infallibilis Deus* (December 8, 1854), in *Pii IX Acta* 1 (1854): 597; Pius XII, Apostolic Constitution *Munificentissimus Deus* (November 1, 1950), in *AAS* 42 (1950): 753-754.

[114] Claudio García Extremeño, O.P., "El sentido de la fe criterio de tradición," in *La Ciencia Tomista* 87 (1960): 569-605 at 603.

it corrections, approval or rejection of beliefs; 3) fully *obey* its final decisions when they are clearly expressed.

However, the *sensus fidei* can prompt the faithful, in exceptional cases, to refuse their assent to some ecclesiastical documents and even to take up, with regard to the supreme authorities, a position of resistance or of apparent disobedience. The disobedience is only apparent, because in these cases of legitimate resistance the principle that we must obey God rather than men applies (Acts 5:29). If we admit the possibility of doctrinal error in documents of the Magisterium, a possibility that cannot be ruled out in principle, there is no doubt that even in the doctrinal field there will be room for these serious cases of conscience.[115]

St. Thomas Aquinas, in several of his works, teaches that, in extreme cases, it is lawful and also a duty to publicly resist a papal decision, as St. Paul resisted St. Peter to his face.

> If the faith were endangered, a subject ought to rebuke his prelate even publicly. Hence Paul, who was Peter's subject, rebuked him in public, on account of the imminent danger of scandal concerning faith, and, as the gloss of Augustine says on Galatians 2:11, "Peter gave an example to superiors, that if at any time they should happen to stray from the straight path, they should not disdain to be reproved by their subjects."[116]

An attitude of resistance when confronted with a teaching of the ecclesiastical authorities which involves a danger to the faith, should be understood not as "disobedience" but, on the contrary, as loyalty and deeper union with the Church and Tradition. However, it must be very clear that no Tradition is possible without apostolic succession, because Christ entrusted only to the apostles and to their legitimate successors the task of transmitting His word. The mistake of the Eastern schismatics was precisely that of disavowing the primacy

---

[115] See, for example, the manifesto of Plinio Corrêa de Oliveira, "A política de distensão do Vaticano com os governos comunistas: Para a TFP: ometir-se ou resistir," in *Catolicismo* 280 (aprile 1974): 4-5; Italian translation "La politica vaticana di distensione verso i governi comunisti," in *Cristianità* 2/5 (maggio-giugno 1974): 7-9, published in 57 daily newspapers in 11 countries, and the letter sent on November 21, 1983, by Abp. Marcel Lefebvre and Bp. Antonio de Castro Mayer to Pope John Paul II concerning some errors of the New Code of Canon Law and of the ceremonies performed on the occasion of the Fifth Centenary of Luther (Bernard Tissier de Mallerais, *Marcel Lefebvre: Une vie* [Estampes: Clovis, 2002] 559-560).

[116] St. Thomas Aquinas, *Summa theologiae*, II-II, q. 33, art. 4, ad 2.

of the Church of Rome in the name of Tradition. But it is equally clear that the successors of the apostles are not free to move away from Tradition, because in that case the *sensus fidei* would give the faithful every right to consider themselves dispensed from obedience.

Then, the fact that assent is suspended on some ecclesiastical documents, certainly does not mean, as firmly stated by the Instruction of the Congregation for the Doctrine of the Faith, *Donum Veritatis* (no. 24), that the Magisterium of the Church can habitually be deceived in its judgments or not enjoy the divine assistance in the integral exercise of its mission. However, *Donum Veritatis* recalls the existence of the *sensus fidei* which "implies then by its nature a profound agreement of spirit and heart with the Church…as God's gift which enables one to adhere personally to the truth, it cannot err" (no. 35).

Moreover, law in the Church is not simply founded on the arbitrary use of power. "On the contrary," canonists observe, "even power in the Church must be just, and this is required by the nature of the Church itself, which determines the purposes and the limits of the activity of the hierarchy. Not each and every act of the sacred Pastors is just merely because it comes from them."[117] Among the injustices possibly committed by the hierarchy, we must first of all distinguish those that affect the individual person and those regarding the common good of the Church. Among the latter, the most serious are those that affect faith or morals and thus endanger the good of the souls. In this last-mentioned case, to withhold assent and to resist may be not only a right, but a duty, as Church history teaches us in countless cases. In turn, this resistance can express itself in a public or a private form. No author has ever raised doubts regarding the right to private opposition to unjust orders, inspired by the same words of St. Peter: "We must obey God rather than men" (Acts 5:29).[118] Legitimate "disobedience" to an order that is unjust in itself

---

[117] Carlos Errázuriz, *Il diritto e la giustizia nella Chiesa* (Milan: Giuffré, 2000), 157.
[118] On private resistance to decisions by the pope or by the Roman Congregations see: St. Thomas Aquinas, *Commentum in IV Librum Sententiarum Magistri Petri Lombardi*, in *Opera omnia* (Paris: Vivés, 1856-1878), X, dist. 19, q. 2, art. 2; idem; *Summa theologiae* II-II, q. 33, art. 4; Francisco Suarez, S.J., *Defensio Fidei Catholicae*, in: *Opera omnia*, XXIV, lib. IV, cap. VI, nos. 14-18; Joachim Salaverri, S.J., *De Ecclesia Christi*, in: *Sacrae Theologiae Summa* (Madrid: BAC, 1958) 1:725-726.

in matters of faith or morals can be taken, in particular cases, to the point of public resistance to the Supreme Pontiff. Arnaldo Xavier da Silveira has proven this clearly in his studies, reporting citations of saints, Doctors of the Church and distinguished theologians and canonists.[119]

According to the words of St. Paul: *"Nos autem sensum Christi habemus"* ["We have the mind of Christ"] (1 Cor. 2:16), as a baptized Christian, every believer has that *sensus fidei* that allows him to express his judgment on what the Church has defined and Tradition has transmitted. Common sense allows him to express, on the level of logic, judgments of fact regarding theological truths also; the *sensus fidei* allows him to express similar judgments in matters of faith: judgments that obviously are not infallible, yet help to form that consensus of the faithful which is one of the *"loci theologici"* through which the Tradition of the Church is maintained.

The Code of Canon Law currently in force, from Canon 208 to Canon 223, under the title *"De omnium christifidelium obligationibus et iuribus"* ["The Obligations and Rights of All Christ's Faithful"] describes the state in life common to all the faithful and attributes to the laity the responsibility to intervene in the problems of the Church. Canon 212 declares that the faithful "have the right, indeed at times the duty, in keeping with their knowledge, competence and position, to manifest to the sacred Pastors their views on matters which concern the good of the Church. They have the right also to make their views known to others of Christ's faithful, but in doing so they must always respect the integrity of faith and morals, show due reverence to the pastors and take into account both the common good and the dignity of individuals."

17. Infallibility of Councils?

What remains to be examined at this point is the relationship of the Councils to Tradition. The Councils are assemblies of bishops who gather to deliberate on ecclesiastical matters. As an expression of the teaching Church they are certainly a "theological source," but they must be classified, based on their importance, as General (or

---

[119] See the series of articles by Arnaldo Xavier da Silveira translated into Italian by the journal *Cristianità* 9 (1975): 3-7; 10 (1975): 11-13; 13 (1975): 6-9.

Ecumenical) Councils,[120] provincial councils, and diocesan councils. General Councils approved by the pope cannot err when they address the Universal Church and express the intention to define a truth, even through a censure of heresy, or excommunication imposed on those who hold a contrary opinion. Their authority derives from being convened, presided over, and ratified by the Roman Pontiff.

Fr. Melchior Cano, in the fourth question of his chapter on the authority of Councils, sets out to establish the method and criterion by which to confirm that the decrees of a Council are certain in matters of faith.[121] The first condition needed to speak about the infallibility of a Council is that its acts must be approved by the Supreme Pontiff; but this is not sufficient, Cano explains, because it is necessary to verify with great care "what is the nature of the matters being judged and what is the meaning and weight of the words."[122] The Dominican theologian thus clearly identifies the signs that help us understand whether the judgments of a Council must be held *de fide*.

> The first and clearest is considering those who affirm the contrary to be heretics...The second sign is when the Synod states its decrees with this formula: "If anyone should opine this or that, let him be anathema." ...The third is if those who say the contrary are condemned *ipso iure*, with a sentence of excommunication... The fourth is if it is stated explicitly and precisely that something must be believed firmly by the faithful or that it is to be accepted as a dogma of Catholic Faith—or similar wording—that something is contrary to the Gospel or to the teaching of the apostles. However, if it is stated—I clarify—not as opinion, but with a firm and certain decree.[123]

If the will to define is lacking or is not expressed clearly, the teaching of a Council cannot be considered infallible, even if approved by the pope, unless it confirms previous doctrinal pronouncements. The supreme authority, Scheeben and the Roman theologians confirm,

---

[120] St. Robert Bellarmine makes a fourfold division of "General" or "Ecumenical Councils," distinguishing between "*approbata; reprobata; partim confirmata – partim reprobata* and *nec manifeste probata, nec manifeste reprobata*" ["approved; rejected; partly confirmed/partly rejected; and neither plainly approved nor plainly rejected"] (*De Conciliis et Ecclesia,* Lib. I, cap. V-VIII, in *De Controversiis christianae fidei, op. cit.,* II, coll. 4-12).

[121] Melchior Cano, *op. cit.,* 327 ff.

[122] *Ibid.,* 328.

[123] *Ibid.,* 328-329.

must clearly express (1) his intention to define, with terms such as *pronuntiamus*, *declaramus*, or *docemus* [We pronounce, We declare, We teach], and (2) his will to bind the faithful.[124]

An Ecumenical Council cannot be transformed into a dogma of faith. The divine gift of infallibility, for a Council as for a pope, pertains only to doctrinal teaching presented in an authoritative and defining manner. The authentic Magisterium of a Council, even if not infallible, demands a certain religious assent of the intellect and will of the faithful, but this assent, as we have seen, is neither irrevocable nor unconditional.

In the instruction of the teaching body of a Council, inaccuracies, ambiguities, obscurities and even nearly heretical or heretical expressions may be found, as happened in the decree *Haec Sancta* of the Council of Constance (1415), solemnly approved by the Council Fathers and ratified by more than one Roman Pontiff. According to Fr. Melchior Cano, that document must instead be rejected because what was approved in that "session" did not have the dogmatic formulation of a "decree in which the faithful were obliged to believe or the contrary was condemned."[125] Similarly, Cardinal Baudrillart, in the *Dictionnaire de Théologie Catholique*, maintains that the Council of Constance did not have the intention of promulgating a dogmatic definition when it published *Haec Sancta*, and this is another reason why that document was later repudiated by the Church.[126]

History serves to remind us that what happened yesterday can happen again today and that, in the past as in the present and future, only one rule remains in times of crisis and difficulty for the Church: fidelity to the Tradition, which is fidelity to the truths entrusted by Christ to His Church with these words: "Heaven and earth will pass away, but my words will not pass away" (Mt. 24:35).

It is necessary to recall that the Councils, as events, must be distinguished from their doctrinal documents. There have been 21

---

[124] Matthias Joseph Scheeben, *Handbook of Catholic Dogmatics, op. cit.,* no. 453.
[125] Melchior Cano, *op. cit.*, 351. Along the same lines, see St. Robert Bellarmine, *De Conciliis*, Lib. II, cap. XIX, coll. 94-96.
[126] A. Baudrillart, article "Concile de Constance," in: DTC, III/1, cols. 1200-1224 at 1221.

Ecumenical Councils in the history of the Church.[127] Some of these are unforgettable because of the theological import of their documents: Nicaea, Trent, Vatican I; others are forgotten, which does not mean that they were not authentic and solemn Councils. A Council goes down in history for the quality of the documents that it produced. In the 16th century there were two Councils: the Fifth Lateran Council (1512-1517) and the Council of Trent (1545-1563). The only dogmatic definition of the Fifth Lateran Council was that the human soul is individual and immortal. The solemn assembly was unable to defuse Protestantism: several months after its conclusion Martin Luther posted his 95 theses in Wittenberg. Everyone remembers the great Council of Trent; no one remembers the Fifth Lateran Council which, in this regard, liked other Councils, can be described as a "failed" Council.

The Second Vatican Council produced documents, but it is not itself a document: like every Council, it is first and foremost an event, a historical moment of the Church which, as such, is situated on the level of facts and not truths. While dogma formulates a truth, which once formulated transcends history, so to speak, Councils are born and die within history and can be judged by historians.

A Council can promulgate dogmas, truths, decrees, or canons which are issued by the Council but are not the Council, and they become part of Tradition only if they are infallibly promulgated or in conformity with the Tradition of the Church. The Council is therefore a part; Tradition is the whole, because, like Sacred Scripture, it is not an event but a source of Revelation.

Affirming the superiority of the Council—of any Council—over Tradition makes no logical sense, much less theological sense. No Council, not even Trent or Vatican I, is greater than Tradition. Tradition must be accepted in its entirety, but the demand to accept a

---

[127] The number of Ecumenical Councils has been debated over the course of Church history. For example, in the late 1500's an ecclesiastical commission met to draw up a list of them, and Cardinal Baronio, considered the great Church historian of his time, had ideas on the subject different from those of Cardinal Robert Bellarmine, whose theses then prevailed. See Johannes Grohe, "Cesare Baronio e la polemica sui Concili ecumenici," in: *Venti secoli di storiografia ecclesiastica: Bilancio e prospettive*, ed. Luis Martínez Ferrer, Acts of the 12th International Convention of the Faculty of Theology *La storia della Chiesa nella storia*, Rome, 13-14 March 2008 (Rome: Edusc, 2010), 131-146.

Council wholesale makes no sense, transforming the historical event into an infallible dogma.

18. The Meaning of "Universal Magisterium"

It would be a serious error to reduce the Church's infallibility to the extraordinary Magisterium of the Roman Pontiff, united with the bishops or not. Even the ordinary Magisterium has a kind of infallibility of its own, under certain conditions. The Church does not have the guarantee of infallibility for every act of her Magisterium, but she cannot err when reaffirming and confirming the same teaching consistently over time.

However, those who maintain that all of the concluding documents of a Council, taken together, enjoy the infallibility which the Spirit of Truth guarantees to the ordinary Magisterium of the Church, demonstrate their inability to distinguish the infallibility of the ordinary Magisterium from that of the extraordinary Magisterium. The reason is that the extraordinary Magisterium of the Church, exercised by the pope alone or in union with the bishops, is infallible even when episodic; the ordinary Magisterium, in contrast, is infallible only in its continuity, not in the sense that continuity over time is in itself the cause of its infallibility, but because this consistent and coherent teaching attests to and makes explicit the existence of a truth that is present in the deposit of faith. Cardinal Bertone explained this in a clear article that he wrote in 1996: the Magisterium can teach a doctrine as definitive with a defining act by a pope or a Council, or by a non-defining act of the ordinary Magisterium, provided that this doctrine is "consistently preserved and held by Tradition and transmitted by the ordinary and universal Magisterium."[128]

Thus, with regard to the co-redemption of the Blessed Virgin Mary, Fr. José de Aldama writes: "While the ordinary Magisterium of the Roman Pontiff is not of itself infallible, if however he teaches a certain doctrine consistently and for an extended period of time to the entire Church, as in our case [of Marian co-redemption], its infallibility must be absolutely admitted; otherwise, the Church

---

[128] Tarcisio Bertone, "A proposito della recezione dei Documenti del Magistero e del dissenso pubblico," in: *L'Osservatore Romano*, 20 dicembre 1996.

would lead the faithful into error."¹²⁹ Consequently, according to Fr. Aldama, the co-redemption of the Virgin Mary is a doctrine already infallibly taught by the Church today, although it has not yet been the subject of any extraordinary proclamation, either pontifical or universal.

In addition to the teaching identified by Fr. de Aldama, others could be mentioned such as the teaching defined in the Encyclical *Humanae Vitae* by Paul VI[130] or by the Apostolic Letter *Ordinatio Sacerdotalis* by John Paul II, which reaffirms the invalidity of priestly ordination of women. Responding to a request for clarification, the Congregation for the Doctrine of the Faith, with a document dated October 28, 1995, in fact confirmed that the doctrine that the Church does not have the ability to confer priestly ordination on women, which is contained in *Ordinatio Sacerdotalis* by John Paul II, "is to be understood as belonging to the deposit of faith."[131] "This teaching," the Vatican document reads, "requires definitive assent, since, founded on the written Word of God, and from the beginning constantly preserved and applied in the Tradition of the Church, it has been set forth infallibly by the ordinary and universal Magisterium."[132]

In these cases we are dealing with the infallibility of the ordinary Magisterium because of the continuity of one and the same teaching through the centuries. The doctrinal foundation of this type of infallibility is as indicated by Fr. de Aldama: if the popes and the universal Church could be deceived in a long and uninterrupted series of ordinary documents concerning the same point, then the gates of hell would prevail against the Bride of Christ. She would be

---

[129] Josephus de Aldama, S.J., "Mariologia," in: *Sacrae Theologiae Summa* (Madrid: BAC, 1961), 3:418.

[130] Ermenegildo Lio, *Humanae Vitae e infallibilità* (Vatican City: Libreria Editrice Vaticana, 1986), *passim*. See also the relevant observations by Fr. Claude Barthe, *L'infaillibilité du pape après Vatican II: Charisme de Pierre et college des évêques* (Paris: Catholica, 1993).

[131] Congregation for the Doctrine of the Faith, *Responsum ad Propositum Dubium* Concerning the Teaching Contained in *Ordinatio Sacerdotalis*, http://www.vatican.va/roman_curia/congregations/cfaith/documents/rc_con_cfaith_doc_19951028_dubium-ordinatio-sac_en.html [accessed 4/21/18].

[132] *Ibid.*, referencing Second Vatican Council, Dogmatic Constitution *Lumen Gentium*, November 21, 1964, no. 25.

transformed into a teacher of errors, whose dangerous influence the faithful would be unable to escape.

In this sense, John Paul II affirms that "the universal ordinary Magisterium...can truly be considered as the usual expression of the Church's infallibility,"[133] and the doctrinal commentary on the Concluding Formula of the *Professio fidei* by the Congregation for the Doctrine of the Faith (June 29, 1998)[134] reaffirms that a doctrine is to be held as infallible when, even without a solemn form of definition, "this doctrine, belonging to the inheritance of the *depositum fidei*, is taught by the ordinary and universal Magisterium" (no. 9). The ordinary universal Magisterium, as the Congregation for the Doctrine of the Faith explains, in order to be considered infallible must be "understood in a diachronic and not necessarily merely synchronic sense."[135] This is why, Cardinal Bertone writes, "in the Encyclicals *Veritatis Splendor* and *Evangelium Vitae* and in the Apostolic Letter *Ordinatio sacerdotalis* itself, the Roman Pontiff intended, though not in a solemn form, to confirm and reaffirm doctrines which belong to the ordinary and universal Magisterium, and which are therefore to be held definitively and unequivocally." "This means," he goes on to explain, "that the morally unanimous consent embraces all eras of the Church, and only by listening to this totality can one remain in the fidelity of the apostles,"[136] citing at this point Cardinal Ratzinger: "A majority that formed at some juncture against the faith of the Church of all times would be no majority."[137]

The term "universal" should therefore be understood in its full extent, not just in space but especially in time, as continuity with the Tradition. It is impossible to consider the Magisterium universal, not

---

[133] John Paul II, Address to the bishops from the U.S.A. on their "Ad limina" visit (15 October 1988). https://w2.vatican.va/content/john-paul-ii/en/speeches/1988/october/documents/hf_jp-ii_spe_19881015_usa-ad-limina.html

[134] Congregation for the Doctrine of the Faith, Doctrinal Commentary on the Concluding Formula of the *Professio fidei*, June 29, 1998, no. 9, http://www.vatican.va/roman_curia/congregations/cfaith/documents/rc_con_cfaith_doc_1998_professio-fidei_en.html [accessed 7/14/18].

[135] Congregation for the Doctrine of the Faith, Doctrinal Commentary on the Concluding Formula of the *Professio fidei*, June 29, 1998, no. 9, http://www.vatican.va/roman_curia/congregations/cfaith/documents/rc_con_cfaith_doc_1998_professio-fidei_en.html [accessed 7/14/18].

[136] Tarcisio Bertone, "A proposito della recezione dei Documenti," *op. cit.*

[137] Joseph Ratzinger, *Called to Communion: Understanding the Church Today*, translated by Adrian Walker (San Francisco: Ignatius Press, 1991), 99.

only when it is delimited in space, but also when it is episodic in time. What is Catholic, which is to say universal? Not something that in a given moment is believed by all "in every place," as might occur in a Council, but rather something that is believed by all always and everywhere. "Always" means without interruption, without ambiguity, without contradiction. "Catholic, or universal," Monsignor Gherardini explains, "and therefore the object of an essentially identical consensus in every corner of the earth, without any interruption of continuity, by the Christians of yesterday, today, and tomorrow."[138]

This is the concept of universality that Vincent of Lérins presents as a sure and normative criterion for distinguishing the truth of the Catholic Faith in an age of errors and heresies, writing:

> Moreover, in the Catholic Church itself, all possible care must be taken, that we hold that Faith which has been believed everywhere, always, by all. For that is truly and in the strictest sense "Catholic," which, as the name itself and the reason of the thing declare, comprehends all universally. This rule we shall observe if we follow universality, antiquity, consensus. We shall follow universality if we confess that one Faith to be true, which the whole Church throughout the world confesses; antiquity, if we in no wise depart from those interpretations which it is manifest were notoriously held by our holy ancestors and fathers; consensus, in like manner, if in antiquity itself we adhere to the consentient definitions and determinations of all, or at the least of almost all priests and doctors.[139]

Recalling the words of St. Paul, "But though we, or an angel from Heaven, preach a gospel to you besides that which we have preached to you, let him be anathema" (Gal. 1:8), the saint of Lérins explains that what St. Paul sets in possible contrast is the objective authority of the Gospel of Christ with the authority of its preachers and interpreters, commenting: "Why does he say 'though we'? Why not rather 'though I'? He means, 'though Peter, though Andrew, though John, in a word, though the whole company of apostles, preach unto you other than we have preached unto you, let him be accursed.' Tremendous severity! He spares neither himself nor his fellow apostles, so he may preserve unaltered the Faith which was at first delivered."[140]

---

[138] Brunero Gherardini, *Quaecumque dixero vobis*, 92.

[139] Vincent of Lerins, *Commonitory*, II, 6 (NPNF-2 11:132b), English translation slightly emended.

[140] Vincent of Lerins, *Commonitory*, VIII, 22 (NPNF-2 11:136b-137a).

The possibility of infidelity to Tradition by an assembly of bishops, rare as it might be, is not ruled out here.

"The Church," Fr. Melchior Cano writes for his part, "is the same and preserves the same Faith that the apostles made known throughout the entire world; and the universality of the Faith today must, without a doubt, be linked to the universality that existed in the Church in past times, going back to the Faith that the apostles spread to the entire world."[141] This is why the oath against modernism of Pope Pius X professes: "I sincerely accept that the doctrine of Faith was handed down to us in the same sense and always with the same meaning from the apostles through the orthodox Fathers."[142]

19. Novelties or development in doctrine?

The Magisterium of the Church, even in its supreme form manifested by the Councils approved by the pope, cannot introduce "novelties," because it is neither creative nor imaginative: it must hold to Scripture and Tradition and must prove that it does so if it does not wish to lose its authority. The First Vatican Council[143] established that the Church cannot add anything to Christian doctrine, because the Revelation which constitutes the object of the Catholic Faith was closed after the death of the last Apostle, and the decree *Lamentabili* by St. Pius X condemned all forms of evolution and novelty of dogma.[144] This is why St. Irenaeus says, "Since the Faith is ever one and the same, neither does one who is able at great length to discourse regarding it, make any addition to it, nor does one, who can say but little, diminish it."[145] Vincent of Lérins explains that there can be development, not in doctrine, but in the knowledge of it. A dogma can be better understood in terms of its scope, clarity, and certainty, but nothing can be added to it. Development, writes St. Vincent in *Commonitorium*, is "in intelligence, knowledge, and wisdom," preserving the same dogma (*in eodem dogmate*), the same sense (*in eodem sensu*), and the same meaning (*in eadem sententia*).[146] It is a

---

[141] Melchior Cano, *op. cit.*, 284.
[142] DH 3537-3550 at 3541.
[143] DH 3011. ["1792" is from an earlier Denzinger edition]
[144] DH 3420-3426.
[145] St. Irenaeus, *Contra Haereses*, I, 10, 2 (ANF 1:331a).
[146] Vincent of Lerins, *Commonitory*, XXIII, 54 (NPNF-2 11:148a).

matter of more clearly expounding what was previously indeterminate and incomplete, or of reinforcing what was already determined and definitive. Pius XII confirms this in his Encyclical *Humani Generis*, affirming that "it is clear how false is a procedure which would attempt to explain what is clear by means of what is obscure. Indeed, the very opposite procedure must be used."[147]

The Dominican theologian Francisco Marín-Sola elucidated the conditions for theological development, but this is neither novelty nor change, because nothing can be added to the deposit of the Faith.[148] Development consists in the passage from implicit to explicit, as noted in the works that preceded the definition of the dogmas of the Immaculate Conception or of the bodily Assumption of the Blessed Virgin Mary. Every time the Church has explicated in new forms the truths contained in the patrimony of the Faith, she has first sought to demonstrate how these were not novelties, but objective truths coming from the Tradition.

20. Vatican Council II and its problems

The Magisterium of the Second Vatican Council is ordinary, authentic, and supreme, and as such it warrants all of our respect and attention, but it is not infallible teaching authority, not because the ordinary Magisterium cannot be infallible, but because it is infallible only when it confirms truth, not when it introduces pastoral or doctrinal novelties.

Infallibility can be present even apart from dogmatic definitions, but it can be deduced only from the criterion of Tradition. The Magisterium of a Council that does not contain dogmatic definitions can be infallible or in any case can teach doctrines that can be described with the theological note of "Catholic doctrine,"[149] only on the condition that that doctrine conforms to the Tradition of the Church, which remains the bedrock of ultimate reference. The adherence "with religious submission of will and intellect to the teachings

---

[147] Pius XII, Encyclical Letter *Humani generis*, August 12, 1950, no. 21, http://w2.vatican.va/content/pius-xii/en/encyclicals/documents/hf_p-xii_enc_12081950_humani-generis.html [accessed 7/14/18].

[148] *Cf.* Francisco Marín-Sola, *L'évolution homogène du Dogme Catholique*, 2 vols. (Fribourg: Oeuvre de St.-Paul, 1924).

[149] Matthias Joseph Scheeben, *Handbook of Catholic Dogmatics*, no. 562.

which either the Roman Pontiff or the College of Bishops enunciate when they exercise their authentic Magisterium, even if they do not intend to proclaim these teachings by a definitive act," required by *Donum veritatis* no. 23 and *Ad tuendam fidem* no. 2, always presupposes the continuity of these documents with Tradition.

What should be done, and was not done, with the most controversial documents of the Council, is precisely this: show their conformity to the Tradition. It is not enough to simply affirm it. The starting point must be the implicit truth of the Faith, believed by the Church, but not yet defined; the end point will be the explication and definition of the truth, and the condemnation of the errors that are opposed to it. This is why development in the understanding of dogma occurs especially in the fight against the errors and heresies that God allows, with the purpose of giving greater prominence to the truth.

The Trinitarian heresies compelled the Church to define theologically the relations between the Persons of the Holy Trinity; the Christological heresies led to clarification of the relationship between the human and divine natures of Christ; the anthropological heresies led to a precise explanation of the connection between grace and freedom in man, and so forth. This is what happened with the Council of Trent which, in order to fight the Protestant conception of the Mass, affirmed the dogma of Transubstantiation, a truth not added to the patrimony of the Faith, but explicated and clarified to counter the heresies. The Magisterium of the Church defines and declares what was earlier believed implicitly and fundamentally, but adds nothing and innovates nothing.

We witnessed the opposite process at the Second Vatican Council: the passage from explicit to implicit, from determined to indeterminate, from clear to confused. This is why there is a need for interpretation and the hermeneutical problem arises. While it is true that in every age Catholic doctrine remains liable to more explicit and pertinent specifications, what the Catholic faithful are asking after Vatican II is to specify clearly and neatly what appears to be equivocal and confusing to them and therefore a source of errors in faith and morals.

The Second Vatican Council, moreover, not only never presented itself as dogmatic, but always described itself—and was described by the popes—as a "pastoral" Council.

There is and should be no contradiction between pastoral and dogmatic, as if the Councils of Nicaea, Trent, or Vatican I were purely dogmatic and not pastoral. So what did the Second Vatican Council intend when it defined itself as pastoral? No more and no less than what John XXIII proclaimed in his inaugural allocution *Gaudet Mater Ecclesia* on October 11, 1962.[150] The Council had been convened not to condemn errors or to formulate new dogmas, but to propose, with a new language, "the truths that are contained in our venerable doctrine." This was theoretically legitimate, and this was why many conservatives enthusiastically participated in the pope's initiative. The Council appeared to them to be an extraordinary opportunity to renew the Church. What happened in reality is that the Johannine "primacy" of pastoral ministry was interpreted in a way similar to the Marxist categories of the "primacy of praxis." The pastoral dimension, which in itself is accidental and secondary with respect to the doctrinal dimension, became the top priority, creating a revolution not primarily in content but in style, language, and mentality.[151] This was expressed in the drafting of ambiguous and ambivalent documents that can be read both in continuity and in discontinuity with Tradition. Even those who accept or propose the "hermeneutic of continuity," that is, who maintain the possibility or necessity of reading the conciliar documents in light of Tradition, must admit however that hermeneutic ambiguity is not an advantage but a shortcoming of the conciliar documents. And the existence of a hermeneutic ambiguity is proven by the ongoing debate.[152] As an ancient legal adage affirms: *in claris non fit interpretatio*; "in clarity there is no room for interpretation."

---

[150] Giovanni XXIII, Discorso dell'11 ottobre 1962, in: *AAS* 54 (1962): 792; see the analysis by Paolo Pasqualucci in: *Giovanni XXIII e il Concilio Ecumenico Vaticano II* (Albano Laziale/Rome: Ichtys, 2008).

[151] Alessandro Gnocchi and Mario Palmaro develop this point nicely in *La Bella addormentata: Perché dopo il Vaticano II la Chiesa è entrata in crisi: Perché si risveglierà* (Florence: Vallecchi, 2011).

[152] See for example the essays by Fr. Giovanni Cavalcoli, O.P. and Fr. Serafino Lanzetta, F.I., in: "Il Vaticano II: In dialogo in modo critico," in: *Fides Catholica* 1 (2011): 207-232, and the debate on the topic hosted by the website of Sandro Magister, www.chiesa.espresso.repubblica.it.

21. The Council in the light of Tradition

The hermeneutic of continuity can be understood in only one way: by reading the documents of the Council in light of the preceding Magisterium of the Church, through a precise method. Wherever ambiguities, uncertainties, or contradictory points are detected, Tradition should be taken as the reference point.[153]

Indeed, not all documents promulgated by the highest ecclesiastical authorities have the same value from a theological perspective. If Benedict XVI expresses certain opinions, as in his books *Jesus of Nazareth* or *Light of the World*,[154] it is obvious that such opinions should be received with the utmost respect because the person speaking is, after all, the Vicar of Christ. But since he himself attributes the value of mere personal opinions to these statements, it is likewise obvious that there is a difference in degree of authority between these and the definition of a dogma, such that these opinions do not demand that same degree of religious assent by the faithful.

The Second Vatican Council, as a solemn meeting of the bishops united with the pope, proposed authentic teachings that were certainly not lacking in authority. Its Magisterium is authentic and supreme. But only those ignorant of theology—and lacking even elementary common sense—could attribute a degree of "infallibility" to all of its teachings.[155]

The claim that the Second Vatican Council must be understood in continuity with the Magisterium of the Church in fact presupposes the existence of doubtful or ambiguous passages in the conciliar documents, which require an interpretation. For Benedict XVI, the

---

[153] In the sense spelled out, for example, by Abp. Marcel Lefebvre in *Vi transmetto quello che ho ricevuto: Tradizione perenne e future della Chiesa* (Milan: Sugarco, 2010), 91.

[154] Benedict XVI, *Light of the World: The Pope, the Church, and the Signs of the Times*, translated by Michael J. Miller and Adrian Walker (San Francisco: Ignatius Press, 2010).

[155] Monsignor Brunero Gherardini identifies in the Second Vatican Council four different levels: a) the general level of the Ecumenical Council as an Ecumenical Council; b) the specific level of the pastoral emphasis; c) the appeal to other Councils; and d) the innovations (*Concilio Vaticano II: Il discorso mancato* [Turin: Lindau, 2011], 90). For a more extensive evaluation of the Council, see *Concilio Ecumenico Vaticano II: Un discorso da fare*, with a preface by His Excellency Mario Olivieri, Bishop of Albenga-Imperia, and an introduction by Cardinal Albert Malcolm Ranjith, Secretary of the Congregation for Divine Worship and the Discipline of the Sacraments (Frigento: Casa Mariana, 2009).

criterion of interpretation for the doubtful passages can only be the Tradition of the Church, as he himself has often reaffirmed. If we wanted to turn the method on its head and affirm that continuity should be interpreted by taking the Council and not Tradition as the reference point, that is, if we wanted to read Tradition in light of the Council and not the other way around, we would need to attribute to the Council that quality of infallibility that no document of the Council has ever had in itself, and then we would need to seek the infallibility of the Council in the event itself, in its spirit, in the impalpable charism that inspires the texts without being translated into defining formulas. But this is exactly the position that Benedict XVI condemned in his address to the curia on December 20, 2005, criticizing the hermeneutic of discontinuity, precisely because it attributes primacy to the spirit over the texts.

There is no need for a theological degree to understand that, in the unhappy event of a conflict—real or apparent—between the "living Magisterium" and Tradition, the primacy can be attributed to Tradition alone, for one simple reason: Tradition, which is the "living" Magisterium considered in its universality and continuity, is infallible in itself, whereas the so-called "living" Magisterium, understood as the current preaching of the ecclesiastical hierarchy, is infallible only under certain conditions. This is why Scheeben affirmed that "The *documents of the ecclesial Tradition of the past* are an autonomous rule only insofar as they are contrasted with the ecclesial preaching of the *present day*; for since they existed *before* the latter, they are also authoritative *for* it."[156] Scheeben adds that in these cases one could also conceive of a sort of *regula fidei* [rule of faith] and even a "*living rule*," which has a sort of relative independence and logical priority with respect to the teaching authority, especially with respect to juridical decisions of the Church: "One such rule is the *sensus omnium fidelium et doctorum* [mind of all the faithful and doctors], insofar as it is understood as the echo of the previous ecclesial preaching or also as the testimony of the Holy Ghost working throughout the Church. But this rule is therefore not the law of faith itself nor the actual promulgation thereof, but only a *testimony* for its existence hitherto and its divine origin."[157]

---

[156] Matthias Joseph Scheeben, *Handbook of Catholic Dogmatics, op. cit.*, no. 414.2.
[157] *Ibid.*, no. 414.3.

Indeed Tradition, which is one of the two sources of the Word of God (the other is Sacred Scripture), is always divinely assisted; the Magisterium is assisted only when it is expressed in the extraordinary form, or when, in the ordinary form, it teaches with continuity over time a truth of faith and morals. The fact that the ordinary Magisterium cannot continuously teach any truth contrary to the Faith does not preclude the same Magisterium from falling *per accidens* into error, when its teaching is circumscribed in space and time and not expressed in extraordinary form. The existence of a divergence between Tradition and the current preaching of the men of the Church can be evidenced precisely by the existence of controversies and the lack of assent and reception by the *sanior pars* [healthier part] of the faithful people.

The "hermeneutic of continuity" recalled by Benedict XVI, therefore, cannot be understood as anything other than an interpretation of the Second Vatican Council in the light of Tradition, or in the light of the divine and apostolic teaching that endures through all ages and is never interrupted. In the Church, in fact, the "rule of faith" is neither the Second Vatican Council, nor the contemporary living Magisterium in terms of its non-definitive content, but rather the perennial Magisterium that constitutes, with Sacred Scripture, one of the two sources of the Word of God. Scripture enjoys inerrancy, and Tradition benefits from the special supernatural assistance of the Holy Ghost.[158] If it were instead granted that Vatican II is the hermeneutic criterion for reinterpreting Tradition, it would paradoxically become necessary to attribute interpretive power to that which is in need of interpretation. Either you maintain that the Council's teachings which cannot be traced back to previous definitions are neither infallible nor irreformable, and therefore not even binding, or else you assign such great authority to the Council that it obscures the other 20 preceding assemblies of the Church, abrogating and replacing them all.

---

[158] Brunero Gherardini, *Quod et tradidi vobis*, 342; *idem*, *Quaecumque dixero vobis*, 175.

22. Apologia for Tradition

Tradition has always been hated by the Church's enemies, both internal and external, because it is the supreme rule of the Catholic Faith: a rule that measures and is not measured, founded on the very Words of Jesus Christ communicated to His Mystical Body, from generation to generation, thanks to the influence of the Holy Ghost; the norm of faith infallibly taught by the pope and by the pastors united with him, and infallibly believed by the faithful people.

Let no one claim that by this defense of Tradition we run the risk of promoting interpretive anarchy. Confusion and anarchy already reign in the Church, unfortunately, and these pages were written precisely in the hope of helping to end the confusion. We know full well that only one supreme and solemn voice can put a stop to the process of self-destruction that is unfolding: the voice of the Roman Pontiff, the only one to whom the power to define the Word of Christ has been guaranteed; he thus becomes the infallible spokesman for Tradition.[159] The area in which the Supreme Pontiff can exercise his infallibility is vast, because it includes all theological and moral questions, excluding none. Morality also includes the political doctrine of the Church regarding society, because, as Pius XII teaches, "good or evil in souls also depends on and is insinuated by the form given to society, in accordance with divine laws or not."[160]

No one can dare to oppose the Vicar of Christ when he exercises his authority. The infallibility of his Magisterium, together with his universal Primacy of governance, is the foundation on which Jesus Christ instituted His Church and on which it will remain firm, by divine promise, until the end of time. But the pope must do this by fulfilling the conditions of the First Vatican Council, in a solemn and defining manner, obliging the faithful to believe what he clarifies and defines in the sphere of faith or morals. No equivocation of a hermeneutical or other sort would then be possible.

A new Syllabus, or a new *Professio fidei*, together with the condemnation of current errors, appears increasingly necessary and urgent

---

[159] With this in view, a "Petition to the Holy Father Benedict XVI that he may promote a more in-depth examination of the pastoral Ecumenical Vatican Council II" (in Italian), was presented on September 24, 2011; so far it has been signed by over 50 Catholic scholars (see the text and the signatures at www.riscossacristiana.it).

[160] Pius XII, Radio Message (June 1, 1941), in *Discorsi e Radiomessaggi*, 3:109.

today. But this is not enough. It is necessary for the Supreme Shepherd to exercise, in all its power and breadth, not only his power to teach but also his power to govern, which derives from his Primacy of jurisdiction. The pope's power to govern is *supreme*, because no one is equal to him in the Church; *plenary*, or unlimited in its juridical scope concerning *rebus fidei et morum* [matters of faith and morals]; *universal*, insofar as it extends personally to every individual bishop and each individual believer; and *immediate*, because he can exercise his right to intervene in any sphere, over any person, and at any time.[161] He must exercise his ecclesiastical *potestas*, not only through teaching, but also through the application of penal sanctions against all those who reject Tradition and call revealed truth into question; his holy predecessors Pius V, Pius IX, and Pius X, among many others, exercised their authority in this way.

As simple faithful, members of the Mystical Body, we turn to the Shepherd of Shepherds reigning today to ask him "not to flee for fear of the wolves"[162] and to confirm us in the Faith, by carrying out his mission completely. Only the pope, the Vicar of Christ, can do it, and we renew our veneration of him, convinced that to him—and to him alone—the Keys of Peter have been entrusted, which are capable of loosing and binding in Heaven and on earth (see Mt. 16:18-20). No one can separate us from this rock on which the Church is built and against which the waves crash in vain.

And yet, even if the Vicar of Christ remained silent, the Holy Ghost would never, not even for a moment, cease to assist His Church in which, even in times of defection from the Faith, a number—however small—of shepherds and faithful will always continue to preserve and transmit Tradition. For them the model is the Most Blessed Virgin Mary, who alone kept faith on the Sabbath before the Resurrection.[163] Her heart was, from that moment on, the jewel case

---

[161] Joël-Benoît d'Onorio, *Le Pape et le gouvernement de l'Église* (Paris: Éditions Fleurus-Tardy, 1992), 100.

[162] "Pray for me, that I may not flee for fear of the wolves," Benedict XVI asked during his first Holy Mass in St. Peter's Square. Benedict XVI, Homily at the Mass for the Beginning of the Petrine Ministry of the Bishop of Rome, April 24, 2005, http://w2.vatican.va/content/benedict-xvi/en/homilies/2005/documents/hf_ben-xvi_hom_20050424_inizio-pontificato.html [accessed July 8, 2018].

[163] Fr. Gabriele Roschini, O.S.M., in his *Dizionario di Mariologia* (Rome: Studium, 1961), 488, describes it as a "rather common opinion." Cf. Roberto de Mattei, "Il sabato e la fede di Maria," in *Immaculata Mediatrix* 2 (2003): 271-283.

of the Tradition of the Church.[164] In ages of crisis, Sacred Tradition remains the infallible rule of faith, the criterion for discerning what is Catholic from what is not, the light that illuminates the Church, making resplendent her marks which will never disappear and which make her unfailingly one, holy, Catholic, apostolic, and Roman.

Catholic Tradition lives in the unbreakable **unity** of the Church, which is fidelity to its *lex credendi* and *orandi*, without ever surrendering even one iota of this; it lives in the **holiness** of Grace irrigated by the channels of the Sacraments and by the correspondence to grace of all those who conform their life to the Words of the Gospel; it lives in **catholicity**, which is the universal word addressed by the Church to all people on earth, and constantly spread by those who believe in the exclusive salvific value of this truth; it lives in **apostolicity**, which is the visible presence on earth of the successors of the apostles, with their power of Holy Orders and jurisdiction that does not change and that every other church lacks.

One, holy, Catholic, and apostolic, the Catholic Church is today more than ever Roman, because *romanità* is nothing other than her Tradition lived out in space and time; and she is militant, because she battles on earth, before suffering in Purgatory and triumphing in Heaven: made up of soldiers who, in accordance with the teaching of St. Paul (see 1 Cor. 9:26), make battle the rule of their earthly life. As faithful soldiers of the militant Church, we want only to raise the flag of Catholic Tradition, of which we too are unworthy bearers, but with the certainty of victory in time and eternity.

---

[164] Concerning the heart of Mary, on that Holy Saturday, St. Bonaventure says that God built His Church as though on a mystical stone (*De Nativitate Beatae Virginis Mariae Sermo V*, in *Opera*, 9:717).

Index of Names

A

Acacius of Constantinople, 23, 25
Adelaide, St., 30
Adorno de' Fieschi, Catherine, St., 46
Alaric, 19, 59
Aldama, José de, 101-102
Alés, Adhemar d', 69
Alexander V (Filargo, Pietro), 38-39
Alexander VI (Borgia, Rodrigo), 43-45, 49
Algermissen, Corrado, 46
Amadeus VIII of Savoy, see also Felix V, antipope, 41
Amann, Émile, 19, 22
Ambrose, St., 16
Amerio, Romano, 2, 11
Antoninus, St., 37
Archi, Alfonso, 57
Aristotle, 48
Arius, 13
Athanasius, St., 13-14, 16, 18, 21
Augustine, St., 19-21, 57, 92, 95
Aurelius, 19

B

Bainvel, Jean-Vincent, 69, 81
Balić, Carlo, 89-90
Barbier, Emanuel, 57
Bardy, Gustave, 19
Baronio, Cesare, 28, 100
Barthe, Claude, 102
Bartolomei, Tommaso M., 89, 93
Basil, St., xi, 59
Basil the Macedonian, 27
Baucher, J., 80
Baudrillart, Alfred-Henri-Marie, 99
Belda Plans, Juan, 64, 68
Bellarmine, Robert, St., 14-15, 25-27, 39, 98-100
Benedict IX, see also Theophylactus III of the Counts of Tusculum, 29
Benedict X, see also Mincio di Velletri, Giovanni, 31
Benedict XI, see also Boccasini, Niccolò, 31
Benedict XIII, see also Luna, Pedro, 36, 38, 40
Benedict XIV, see also Lambertini, Prospero, 51
Benedict XVI, see also Ratzinger, Joseph, 1-2, 37-38, 59, 61-63, 84, 88, 93, 109-113
Bernard of Clairvaux, St., 32
Bernardine of Siena, St., 41
Berno of Cluny, Abbot, 29
Bertone, Tarcisio, 98, 100
Bertrand de Got, see also Clement V, 34
Billot, Louis, 25, 74
Blanco, Antonio, 88, 91
Boccasini, Niccolò, see also Benedict XI, 31
Bonaparte, Napoleon, see Napoleon I, Emperor
Bonaventure da Begnoregio, St., 88, 114
Boniface I, St., 19
Boniface IX, see also Tomacelli, Pietro, 36
Boniface VIII, see also Caetani, Benedetto, 34, 63
Bosco, John, St., 56
Bossuet, Jacques-Bénigne, 55
Bracciolini, Giovanni Francesco Poggio, 43
Brandmüller, Walter, 40
Braschi, Gianangelo, see also Pius VI, 53
Breakspear, Nicholas, see Hadrian IV
Brehier, Louis, 19
Bridget of Sweden, St., 35, 37
Bruno di Segni, St., 31
Brunone Lanteri, Pio, 54-55

C

Cabrol, Fernand, 26
Caetani, Benedetto, see also Boniface VIII, 33

Callixtus II, see also Guy of Burgundy, 32
Cano, Melchior, 64-70, 75, 82, 85, 91, 94, 98-99, 105
Cantoni, Giovanni, 43
Cantoni, Pietro, 71
Capitani, Osvaldo, 31
Cappello, Felice Maria, 79
Carafa, Giampaolo, see also Paul IV, 46
Castro Mayer, Antonio de, 95
Catherine of Siena, St., 35, 37, 48
Cavalcoli, Giovanni, 82-83, 108
Celestine I, St., 93
Celestius, 19-20
Cenci, Pio, 5
Cerularius, Michael, 28
Cesarini, Giuliano, 41
Charlemagne, 28, 33
Charles V, 48
Charlier, Louis, 69
Chenu, Marie-Dominique, 69
Chiaramonti, Gregorio, see also Pius VII, 53
Chieregati, Francesco, 47
Chrysologus, Peter, 64
Claeys-Boùùaert, Ferdinand, 79
Clement V, see also Bertrand de Got, 34, 52
Clement VII, see also Giulio de' Medici, 36, 48-49
Clement VII, antipope, see also Robert of Geneva, 36
Clement XIII, see also Rezzonico, Carlo, 50, 53
Clement XIV, see also Ganganelli, Lorenzo, 51
Clodovicus I (Clovis), 23
Cognasso, Francesco, 4
Colonna, Oddone, see also Martin V, 40
Composta, Dario, 79
Condulmer, Gabriele, see also Eugene IV, 40
Congar, Yves, 69, 80
Constans, Emperor, 14-15
Constantin, C., 92
Constantine, Emperor, 12-13, 15, 28, 61
Corecco, Eugenio, 80
Corrêa de Oliveira, Plinio, 43, 93, 95
Correr, Angelo, see Gregory XII

Corsini, Andrea, St., 42
Cossa, Baldassarre, see also John XXIII, 38
Cristiani, Léon, 39
Cunegonde of Luxembourg, 30
Cybo, Giovanni Battista, see also Innocent VIII, 43
Cyprian, St., 19
Cyril of Alexandria, 20, 21, 93
Cyrus of Alexandria, 24

D

d'Onorio, Joël-Benoît, 113
Dal Gal, Girolamo, 57
Damasus, I, St., 15
de Beaufort, Pierre Roger, see Gregory XI
de Grimoard, Guillaume, see Urban V
dei Paganelli, Pietro Bernardo, see Eugene III
de Labriolle, Paul, 19
de' Liguori, Alphonsus Maria, St., 51, 94
de Luca, Antonino, 5
de Luna, Pedro, see also Benedict XIII, 35
de Mattei, Roberto, xiii, 55-56, 93, 113
de' Medici, Giovanni, see also Leo X, 44
de' Medici, Giulio, see also Clement VII, 36, 48-49
de Paul, Vincent, St., 26, 46
de Plinval, Georges, 19
Descartes, René, 82
Dillenschneider, Clément, 93
Diocletian, 12
Dioscuros I of Alexandria, 21
Dominici, Giovanni, 39, 42
Donoso Cortés, Juan, 93
Dublanchy, Edmond, 27
Duèse, Jacques, see John XXII
Duns Scotus, John, Blessed, 93

E

Emiliani, Jerome, St., 46
Errázuriz, Carlos, 96
Esch, Arnold, 7
Eugene I, 24

INDEX OF NAMES

Eugene III, see also dei Paganelli, Pietro Bernardo, 31-32
Eugene IV, see also Condulmer, Gabriele, 40-42
Eusebius of Dorylaeum, 20-21
Eusebius of Vercelli, 16-17
Eutychus, 21-22

F

Facundus of Hermiana, 22
Falco, Giorgio, 39
Farina, Raffaele, 7
Febronius, Justinus, 50
Federico dell'Addolorata, 64, 86
Federico di Lorena, see Stephen IX
Felix V, antipope, see also Amadeus VIII of Savoy, 41
Ferrer, Vincent, St., 37, 42, 100
Fieschi, Sinibaldo dei Conti di Lavagna, see Innocent IV
Filograssi, Giuseppe, 70
Flavianus of Constantinople, 21
Florent, Adrian, see also Hadrian VI, 45-47
Formosus, 28
Fornaseri, G., see Falco Giorgio, 39
Frances of Rome, St., 42
Francis de Sales, St., 46
Francis of Paola, St., 42
Franzelin, Johann Baptist, 16, 75, 85, 90-91

G

Gaetano of Thiene, St., 46
Ganganelli, Lorenzo, see also Clement XIV, 51-53
García Extremeño, Claudio, 94-95
Gardeil, Ambroise, 64
Garrigou-Lagrange, Réginald, 89
Gasparri, Pietro, 79
Gelasius, 23
Gérard of Bourgogne, see Nicholas II
Gherardini, Brunero, 2, 70, 74-76, 80, 83, 104, 109, 111
Ghilardi, Massimiliano, 22
Ghislieri, Michele, see also Pius V, 49
Giovanni, de' Medici, see Leo X
Giovanni di Sabina, see also Sylvester III, 29
Giuliano della Rovere, see also Julius II, 44
Giulio de' Medici, see also Clement VII, 48
Gleize, Jean-Michel, 74, 85, 90
Gnocchi, Alessandro, 108
Gratian, 26
Graziano, Giovanni, see also Gregory VI, 29
Gregory I, see Gregory the Great, St.
Gregory the Great, St., 1, 23
Gregory VI, see also Graziano, Giovanni, 29
Gregory VII, St., see also Ildebrando di Soana, 30-31, 51
Gregory XI, see also de Beaufort, Pierre Roger, 34-35
Gregory XII, see also Correr, Angelo, 36, 38-40
Gregory, XVI, 69
Grignion de Montfort, Louis-Marie, St., 51
Grohe, Johannes, 100
Gualberto, Giovanni, St., 29
Guéranger, Prosper, 20-21, 46, 59
Guy of Burgundy, see Callixtus II

H

Hadrian II, 25-26, 28
Hadrian IV, see also Breakspear, Nicholas, 32
Hadrian VI, see also Florent, Adrian, 46-48
Hefele, Karl Joseph von, 28
Henry I, Emperor, 30
Henry II, St., Emperor, 30
Henry V, Emperor, 31, 54
Henry VIII, King, xii, 49
Heraclius, 22, 24
Hergenröther, Josef, 3-5, 13-15, 19, 21-22, 25, 28-29, 31-34, 38-39, 41-42, 44-45, 50, 54, 58
Hervada, Javier, 78
Hervé, Jean-Marie, 20
Hilary of Poitiers, St., 14, 16-18
Holstein, Henri, 73, 76, 81
Honorius I, 23-26

Hontheim, Johann Nikolaus von, see Febronius, Justinus
Hormisdas, St., 23

I

Ignatius of Loyola, St., 46, 52
Ildebrando di Soana, see also Gregory VII, St., 30-31, 51
Ingeborg, Walter, 31
Innocent III, see also Lotario dei Conti di Segni, 32-33
Innocent IV, see also Fieschi, Sinibaldo dei Conti di Lavagna, 32
Innocent VII, see also Migliorati, Cosimo, 36, 43
Innocent VIII, see also Cybo, Giovanni Battista, 43-44
Innocent XI, see also Odescalchi, Innocenzo, 50
Irenaeus of Lyons, St., 73, 76
Irene, Empress, 27

J

Jansen, 50
Jeanne de Chantal, St., 46
Jedin, Hubert, 3, 31
Jerome, St., 14-15, 21, 46, 58
Jobin, Guy, 82
Joan of Arc, St., 37
John, St., x, 70, 86
John of Capestrano, St., 42
John of God, St., 46
John of Salisbury, 32
John Paul II, see also Wojtyła, Karol, 1, 95, 102-103
John VIII Palaeologus, 41
John XXII, see also Duèse, Jacques, 34
John XXIII, see also Cossa, Baldassarre, 38-39, 61, 108
Joseph II, Emperor, 41, 50
Journet, Charles, 27, 32, 52, 77, 79
Julian the Apostate, 12
Julius I, St., 14
Julius II, see also Giuliano della Rovere, 44
Justinian, Lawrence, St., 42
Justinian I of Byzantium, 22-23

K

Kasper, Walter, 91
Kirsch, Johann Peter, 3-4
Kreuzer, Georg, 26

L

Lambertini, Prospero, see also Benedict XIV, 51
Lang, Albert, 64
Lanteri, Pio Brunone, 54-55
Lanzetta, Serafino, 108
Le Bachelet, Xavier, 13
Lefebvre, Marcel, 95, 109
Leflon, Jean, 54
Leo I, St., see Leo the Great, St.
Leo II, 24-25, 28
Leo III, St., 33
Leo X, see also de' Medici, Giovanni, 44-46, 49
Leo XIII, see also Pecci, Gioacchino, 3-5, 7, 17, 28, 56-57, 63
Leo the Great, St., 1, 21, 23
Le Tourneau, Dominique, 69, 80
Liberius, 14, 16, 22
Lidwina of Schiedam, St., 33
Lio, Ermenegildo, 102
Lotario dei Conti di Segni, see also Innocent III, 32-33
Lucien, Bernard, 70, 77
Ludwig the Bavarian, Emperor, 36
Luther, Martin, 42, 44-45, 82, 95, 100

M

Magister, Sandro, 108
Maistre, Joseph de, 55, 92
Mandonnet, Pierre, 64
Mansi, Giovanni Domenico, 19, 38
Marcian, 21
Marín-Sola, Francisco, 106
Martin, Victor, 27
Martina, Giacomo, 4
Martínez Ferrer, Luis, 100
Martin I, St., 24
Martin V, see also Colonna, Oddone, 40
Mastai Ferretti, Giovanni Maria, see also Pius IX, Blessed, 54

INDEX OF NAMES

Matilda, St., 30
Maxentius, 12
Maximus the Confessor, St., 24
Mayer, Agostino, 22
Merici, Angela, St., 46
Merry del Val, Rafael, 57
Messori, Vittorio, 61-62
Michael III of Byzantium, Emperor, 26
Michel, Albert, 74-75, 81
Migliorati, Cosimo, see also Innocent VII, 36, 43
Millet, Hélène, 39
Mincio di Velletri, Giovanni, see also Benedict X, 31
Minnerath, Roland, 23
Monachino, Vincenzo, 14
Montini, Giovanni Battista, see Paul VI
Mörsdorf, Klaus, 80
Murri, Romolo, 57

N

Napoleon I, Emperor, 53-54
Nau, Paul, 70
Neri, Philip, St., 46
Nero, Emperor, 11
Nestorius, 20-21
Newman, John Henry, xi, 16-17, 20
Nicholas I, St., 26
Nicholas II, see also Gérard de Bourgogne, 31
Nicholas of Cusa, 41
Nicholas V, see also Parentucelli, Tommaso, 43

O

Ocáriz, Fernando, 88, 91
Oddone di Lagery, see Urban II
Odescalchi, Innocenzo, see also Innocent XI, 50
Ohly, Christoph, 87
Olivieri, Mario, 109
Ottaviani, Alfredo, 78-79

P

Pacelli, Eugenio, see Pius XII
Palmaro, Mario, 108
Parente, Pietro, 6, 69-70
Parentucelli, Tommaso, see also Nicholas V, 43
Paschal II (Raineri, Rainerio), 30-32, 54
Pasqualucci, Paolo, 108
Pastor, Ludwig von, 4-5, 35-40, 43-49, 51-53, 56, 58, 60
Paul, St., ix, 11, 58, 72, 74, 78, 95, 97, 104, 114
Paul IV, see also Carafa, Giampaolo, 49
Paul VI, see also Montini, Giovanni Battista, 1, 26, 61-62, 102
Paulinus of Aquileia, St., 22
Paulinus of Trier, St., 14
Paulinus of Nola, St., 18
Pecci, Gioacchino, see Leo XIII
Pelagius, 19-20, 22
Pensabene, Giuseppe, 36
Pero-Sanz, José Miguel, 88
Perrone, Giovanni, 85, 90
Peter, St., 11, 16, 38, 41-42, 48, 60, 69, 72, 78, 86, 95-96, 104
Peter Damian, St., 30-31
Peter of Luxembourg, 37
Philip the Fair, 33-34, 52
Photius of Constantinople, 28
Piccolomini, Enea Silvio, see also Pius II, 41
Pighius, Albert, 26
Pilara, Luca, 22
Piolanti, Antonio, 6
Pitra, Giovanni Battista, 5
Pius II, see also Piccolomini, Enea Silvio, 41
Pius IX, Blessed, see also Mastai Ferretti, Giovanni Maria, 4, 55-57, 77, 93-94, 113
Pius V, St., see also Ghislieri, Michele, 49-51, 113
Pius VI, see also Braschi, Gianangelo, 53
Pius VII, see also Chiaramonti, Gregorio, 4, 52-54
Pius X, St., see also Sarto, Giuseppe, 3, 51, 55, 57, 79, 90, 105, 113
Pius XII, see also Pacelli, Eugenio, 42, 57, 63, 68-70, 77-78, 90, 94, 106, 112
Politi, Vincenzo, 80
Polycarp, St., 76
Pozo Sánchez, Cándido, 64

Prignano, Bartolomeo, see also Urban VI, 36
Prosper of Aquitaine, St., 73
Pulcheria, St., 21
Pyrrhus, 28

R

Ranjith, Albert Malcolm, 109
Ratzinger, Joseph, see also Benedict XVI, 1, 61-62, 103
Rezzonico, Carlo, see Clement XIII
Robert of Geneva, see also Clement VII, antipope, 36
Robert of Lincoln, 32
Rodulfus Glaber, 30
Romuald, St., 29
Roschini, Gabriele, 113
Routhier, Gilles, 82

S

Salaverri, Joachim, 97
Sancho Bielsa, Jesús, 87, 89
Sangnier, Marc, 57
Sarto, Giuseppe, see also Pius X, 3, 51, 55, 57, 79, 90, 105, 113
Scheeben, Matthias Joseph, 18, 72, 75-77, 79-80, 85, 90-91, 99, 106, 110
Schmaus, Michael, 57, 75
Schuster, Ildefonso, Blessed, 34-35
Semeraro, Cosimo, 7
Sergius I, 24
Sigismund of the Holy Roman Empire, 39
Simonetti, Manlio, 14
Sophronius, St., 24
Sordi, Marta, 11
Sotinel, Claire, 22
Soubirous, Bernadette, St., 93
St.-Cyran, Jean Duvergier de Hauranne, Abbot of, 50
Stephen IX, see also Federico di Lorena, 30
Stephen VI, 28
Stickler, Alfons Maria, 78-79
Suarez, Francisco, 97
Sylvester III, see also Giovanni di Sabina, 29

T

Teresa of Avila, St., 46
Tertullian, 12
Testore, Celestino, 4
Theodore, St., 28
Theodosius II, Emperor, 21
Theodosius the Great, Emperor, 15
Theophylactus III of the Counts of Tusculum, see also Benedict IX, 29
Thérèse of Lisieux, St., 93
Thomas Aquinas, St., 38, 56, 79, 86-88, 95, 97
Timothy, 72, 74
Tissier de Mallerais, Bernard, 95
Tomacelli, Pietro, see Boniface IX
Torquemada, Juan, 41

U

Urban II, see also Oddone di Lagery, 30-31
Urban V, see also de Grimoard, Guillaume, 35
Urban VI, see also Prignano, Bartolomeo, 36

V

Valla, Lorenzo, 43
Valverde, Carlos, 93
Vernazza, Ettore, 46
Victor III, 30
Vidal, Pietro, 27, 79
Vidigal Xavier da Silveira, Arnaldo, 26, 97
Vigilius, 22, 25
Viguerie, Jean, 53
Vincent of Lérins, St., x-xi, 104-105
Vitali, Dario, 87

W

Wernz, Francisco Xavier, 27, 79
William of Dijon, St., 29
Wojtyła, Karol, see John Paul II

X

Xavier da Silveria, Arnaldo, see Vidigal
    Xavier da Silveira, Arnaldo

Z

Zaccaria, Anthony Maria, St., 46
Zocca, Elena, 26
Zosimus, 19, 22, 25